AIR PUBLICATION 1565 B
Volume I
AIR MINISTRY.

Royal Air Force

Pilot's Notes

SPITFIRE IIA and IIB AEROPLANES

MERLIN XII ENGINE

by Air Ministry

Prepared by direction of the
Minister of Aircraft Production

Promulgated by order of the Air Council.

©2012 Periscope Film LLC
All Rights Reserved
ISBN#978-1-937684-68-6

Volume I

Pilot's Notes

AMENDMENT CERTIFICATE

Incorporation of an amendment list in this publication should be certified by inserting the amendment list number, initialling in the appropriate column and inserting the date of incorporation.

Holders of the Pilot's Notes will receive only those amendment lists applicable to the preliminary matter, introduction and sections 1 and 2.

Amendt. List No.										
Prelimy. matter										
Leading Partics.										
Introducn.										
Section 1										
Section 2										
Section 3										
Section 4										
Section 5										
Section 6										
Section 7										
Section 8										
Section 9										
Section 10										
Section 11										
Section 12										
Date of incorpn.	INCORPORATED				1 AUG 194					

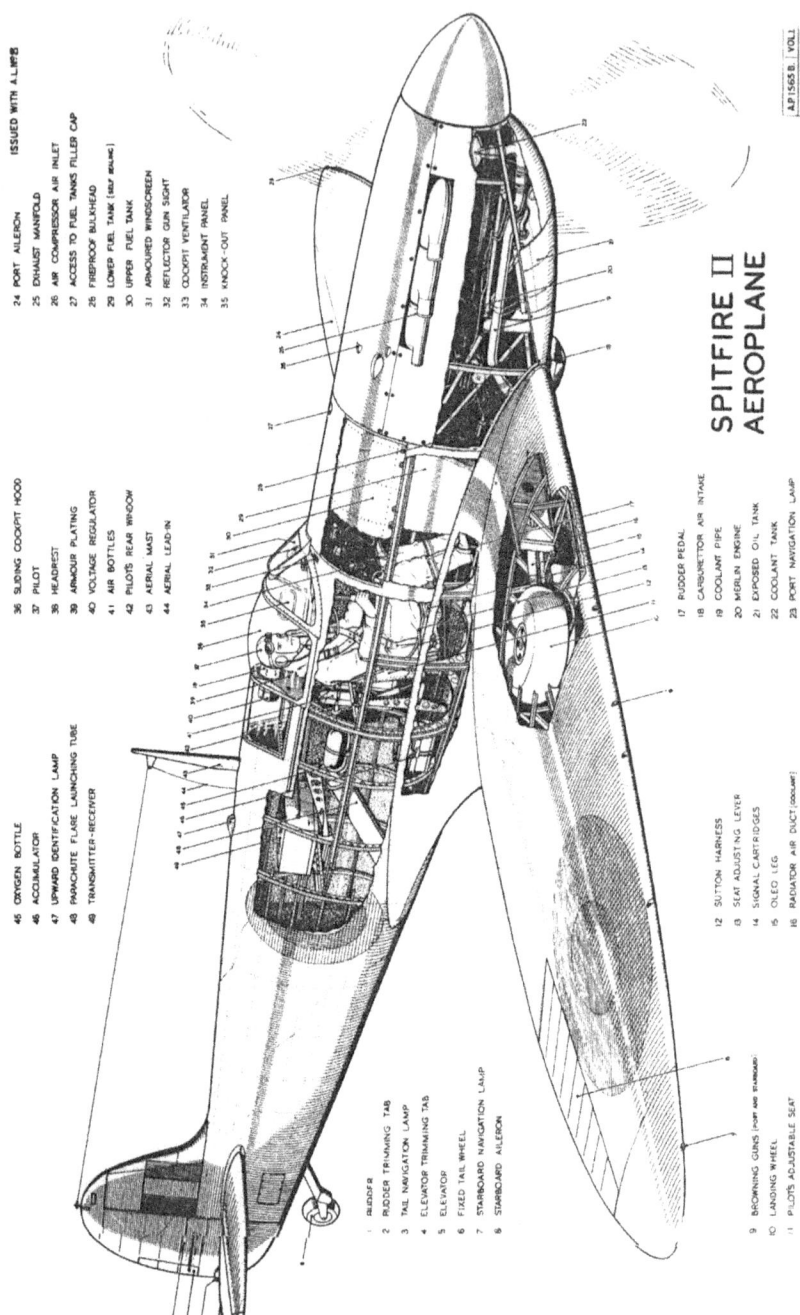

July, 1940

AIR PUBLICATION 1565B
Pilot's Notes

LIST OF SECTIONS

(A detailed Contents List is given at
the beginning of each Section)

Introduction

Section 1 - Pilot's controls and equipment

       2 - Handling and flying notes for pilot

R.T.P./592.3550.6/40

NOTES TO OFFICIAL USERS

Air Ministry Orders and Vol. II leaflets as issued from time to time may affect the subject matter of this publication. It should be understood that amendment lists are not always issued to bring the publication into line with the orders or leaflets and it is for holders of this book to arrange the necessary link-up.

Where an order or leaflet contradicts any portion of this publication, an amendment list will generally be issued, but when this is not done, the order or leaflet must be taken as the overriding authority.

Where amendment action has taken place, the number of the amendment list concerned will be found at the top of each page affected and amendments of technical importance will be indicated by a vertical line on the left-hand side of the text against the matter amended or added. Vertical lines relating to previous amendments to a page are not repeated. If complete revision of any division of the book (e.g. a Chapter) is made this will be indicated in the title page for that division and the vertical lines will not be employed.

July, 1940
AIR PUBLICATION 1565B
Volume I

LIST OF SECTIONS

(A detailed Contents List is given at the beginning of each Section)

Leading Particulars

Introduction

Section 1 — Pilot's controls and equipment
       2 — Handling and flying notes for pilot

Note: Sections 3-11, for ground support personnel, are available separately.

Section 3 — Not applicable
       4 — Instructions and notes for ground personnel

          Chap. 1 — Handling and general preparation
               2 — Maintenance

       5 — Removal and assembly operations
       6 — Electrical installation — Wiring diagrams and maintenance notes
       7 — Design and construction of airframe

          Chap. 1 — Fuselage
               2 — Main planes
               3 — Tail unit
               4 — Flying controls
               5 — Alighting gear

       8 — Engine installation
       9 — Hydraulic and pneumatic systems
     10 — Electrical installation — Description
     11 — Equipment

Note.— Sections or chapters included above but not found in this handbook will be issued by Amendment List at a later date.

R.T.P./592.1275.6/40

*This page re-issued with A.L. No. 30
December, 1943*

A.P.1565B, Vol. I

LEADING PARTICULARS

Name	Spitfire IIA or IIB
Duty	Fighter
Type	Single-seater, low-wing monoplane

MAIN DIMENSIONS
(In flying attitude, datum line horizontal)

Span	36 ft. 10 in.
Length overall	29 ft. 11 in.
Height—to top of propeller	11 ft. 5½ in.
Height to centre of propeller boss	6 ft. 1 in.

Main plane

Aerofoil section	N.A.C.A.2200 series
Chord (mean aerodynamic)	7 ft. 1 in.
Incidence	2° at root
	$-\frac{1}{2}°$ at tip
Dihedral	6°

Tail plane

Span (over elevators)	10 ft. 6 in.
Chord (maximum)	4 ft. 0 in.
Incidence	0°

Fuselage

Width (maximum)	3 ft. 6 in.
Length overall	20 ft. 10 in.
Height (maximum)	6 ft. 9 in.

AREAS

Main plane, including ailerons and flaps	242·0 sq. ft.
Ailerons, total	18·9 sq. ft.
Flaps, total	15·6 sq. ft.
Tail plane, including elevators	31·46 sq. ft.
Elevators, two, with trimming tabs	13·26 sq. ft.
Trimming tabs, total	0·76 sq. ft.
Fin	4·61 sq. ft.
Rudder, with tab	8·23 sq. ft.
Trimming tab	0·35 sq. ft.

CONTROL SURFACES, SETTINGS AND RANGES OF MOVEMENT
(Alternative linear dimensions and tolerances are given in Sect. 4, Chap. 2, fig. 1A)

Tail plane	Fixed horizontal
Fin	Central

F.S./1

B (AL 30)

This page amended by A.L. No. 30
December, 1943

Ailerons (at inboard end)	...	Up 26° Down 19°
Aileron droop	...	⅜ in. on both ailerons
Elevators (at inboard end rib)	...	Up 28° Down 23°
Elevator trimming tabs	...	Up 20° Down 7°
Rudder (at maximum chord)	...	Each way 28°
Rudder trimming tab	...	Each way 12°
Flaps	...	Down 85°

UNDERCARRIAGE

Type	...	Retractable, cantilever
Track	...	5 ft. 8½ in.
Shock-absorber struts—		
Type	...	Vickers oleo-pneumatic, No. 90273
Air pressure (wheels off ground)	...	420 lb./sq. in.
Wheels	...	Dunlop AH.2061
Tyres	...	Dunlop IJ. 12, 13 or 17
Tube	...	IJ. 12, 13 or 17
Tyre pressure	...	51 lb./sq. in.
Brakes	...	Dunlop pneumatic

TAIL WHEEL UNIT

Shock-absorber strut—		
Type	...	Vickers oleo-pneumatic, No. 90356
Air pressure (wheels off ground)	...	215 lb./sq. in.
Wheel	...	Dunlop AH.2184/IX
Tyre	...	Dunlop TA.11, 12 or 14
Tube	...	TA. 2 or 3
Tyre pressure	...	Spitfire IIA 36 lb./sq. in. Spitfire IIB 39 lb./sq. in.

ENGINE

Name	...	Merlin XII
Type	...	12-cylinder V-type liquid-cooled, supercharged
Fuel	...	} See A.P.1464, Vol. II, leaflet C/37
Oil	...	
Coolant	...	70% distilled water, 30% ethylene glycol, Specification D.T.D.344A (Stores Ref. 33C/559)
Fuel pump relief valve spring	...	Part No. D.10310
Oil dilution system—		
Type of valve	...	5U/1513
Voltage of valve	...	12
Fuel pressure on valve	...	2½ lb./sq. in.
Valve orifice diameter	...	0·070 in.

This page amended by A.L. No. 30
December, 1943

TANK CAPACITIES

Fuel tanks—top	48 galls.
—bottom	37 galls.
Total	85 galls.
Oil tank	5·8 galls. oil
	1·75 galls. air space

PROPELLERS

Type	Rotol, RX5/1
Control	Constant speed
Pitch settings	Coarse 63° 10'
	Fine 28° 10'
Diameter of blades	10 ft. 3 in.
Number of blades	3
Material	Magnesium alloy

or

Type	Rotol, RX5/3
Control	Constant-speed
Pitch settings	Coarse 65° 15'
	Fine 30° 15'
Diameter of blades	10 ft. 3 in.
Number of blades	3
Material	Wood (Jablo finish)
Stores Ref.	25A/396

or

Type	de Havilland No. 5/39A
Control	Constant-speed
Pitch settings	Basic 52°
	Coarse 52°
	Fine 32°
Diameter of blades	10 ft. 9 in.
Number of blades	**3**
Material	Dural
Stores Ref.	25A/437

F.S./2

AIR PUBLICATION 1565B

SECTION 1.

CONTROLS AND EQUIPMENT FOR PILOT

LIST OF CONTENTS

	Para.
INTRODUCTION	1
MAIN SERVICES	
Fuel System	2
Oil System	3
Hydraulic System	4
Pneumatic System	5
Electrical System	6
AIRCRAFT CONTROLS	
Primary Flying Controls	7
Flying Instruments	8
Trimming Tabs	9
Undercarriage Controls	10
Flap	11
Undercarriage Emergency Operation	12
Wheel Brakes	13
ENGINE CONTROLS	
Throttle and Mixture	14
Automatic Boost Cut-Out	15
Airscrew	16
Radiator Flap	17
Slow running Cut-Out	18
Fuel Cock and Contents Gauges	19
Fuel Priming Pump	20
Ignition Switches	21
Cartridge Starter	22
Hand Starting	23
Engine Instruments	24
COCKPIT ACCOMMODATION AND EQUIPMENT	
Pilot's Seat Controls	25
Safety Harness Release	26
Cockpit Door	27
Hood Locking Control	28
Direct Vision Panel	29
Cockpit Lighting	30
Cockpit Heating and Ventilation	31
Oxygen	32
Mirror	33
Map Cases	34
OPERATIONAL EQUIPMENT AND CONTROLS	
Guns and Cannon	35
Reflector Gun Sight	36
Camera	37

	Para.
NAVIGATIONAL SIGNALLING AND LIGHTING EQUIPMENT	
Wireless	38
Navigation and Identification Lamps	39
Landing Lamps	40
Signal Discharger	41
DE-ICING EQUIPMENT	
Windscreen	42
Pressure Head	43
EMERGENCY EQUIPMENT	
Hood Jettison	44
Forced Landing Flare	45
First Aid	46

FIGURES

Frontispiece
Port Side of Cockpit Fig 1
Starboard Side of Cockpit Fig 2

NOTES TO OFFICIAL USERS

Air Ministry Orders and Vol. II leaflets as issued from time to time may affect the subject matter of this publication. It should be understood that amendment lists are not always issued to bring the publication into line with the orders or leaflets and it is for holders of this book to arrange the necessary link-up.

Where an order or leaflet contradicts any portion of this publication, an amendment list will generally be issued, but when this is not done, the order or leaflet must be taken as the overriding authority.

Where amendment action has taken place, the number of the amendment list concerned will be found at the top of each page affected, and amendments of technical importance will be indicated by a vertical line on the left-hand side of the text against the matter amended or added. Vertical lines relating to previous amendments to a page are not repeated. If complete revision of any division of the book (e.g. a Chapter) is made this will be indicated in the title page for that division and the vertical lines will not be employed.

Revised December 1941.
Issued with A.L.No.19/F

AIR PUBLICATION 1565B
Volume I and
Pilot's Notes.

SECTION I

PILOT'S CONTROLS AND EQUIPMENT

INTRODUCTION

1. The Spitfire IIA and IIB are single seat, low wing monoplane fighters each fitted with a Merlin XII engine and a de Havilland 20° (P.C.P.) or Rotol 35° constant speed airscrew.

MAIN SERVICES

2. Fuel System -

   Fuel is carried in two tanks mounted one above the other (the lower one is self-sealing) forward of the cockpit and is delivered by an engine driven pump. The tank capacities are as follows:

Top tank:	48 gallons
Bottom tank:	37 gallons

   The top tank feeds into the lower tank, and the fuel cock controls (38 and 39), one for each tank, are fitted below the instrument panel.

3. Oil System -

   Oil is supplied by a tank of 5.8 gallons capacity fitted below the engine mounting, and two oil coolers in tandem are fitted in the underside of the port plane.

4. Hydraulic System -

   An engine-driven hydraulic pump supplies the power for operating the under-carriage.

5. Pneumatic system -

   An engine-driven air compressor feeds two storage cylinders for operation of the flaps, brakes, guns and landing lamps. The cylinders are connected in series, each holding air at 200 lb/sq.in pressure.

6. Electrical System -

   A 12 Volt generator, controlled by a switch (56) above the instrument panel, supplies an accumulator which in turn supplies the whole of the electrical installation. There is a voltmeter (55) on the left of the switch.

F.S/2

Issued with A.L.No.19/F

AEROPLANE CONTROLS

7. **Primary flying controls and locking devices**

    (a) The control column (37) is of the spade-grip pattern and incorporates the brake lever and gun and cannon firing control. The rudder pedals (41) have two positions for the feet and are adjustable for leg reach by rotation of star wheels (42) on the sliding tubes.

    (b) Control locking struts are stowed on the right hand side of the cockpit, behind the seat. To lock the control column, the longer strut should be clamped to the control column handle at one end and the other end inserted in a key-hole slot in the right hand side of the seat. The fixed pin on the free end of the arm attached to this strut at the control column end should then be inserted in a lug (72) on the starboard datum longeron, thus forming a rigid triangle between the column, the seat and the longeron.

    (c) To lock the rudder pedals, a short bar with a pin at each end is attached to the other struts by a cable. The longer of the two pins should be inserted in a hole in the starboard star wheel bearing and the shorter in an eyebolt (77) on the fuselage frame directly below the front edge of the seat. The controls should be locked with the seat in its highest position.

8. **Flying instruments**

    A standard blind flying instrument panel is incorporated in the main panel. The instruments comprise airspeed indicator (28), altimeter (30), directional gyro (31), artificial horizon (29), rate of climb and descent indicator (49), and turn and bank indicator (48).

9. **Trimming tabs**

    The elevator trimming tabs are controlled by a hand wheel (7) on the left hand side of the cockpit, the indicator (21) being on the instrument panel. The rudder trimming tab is controlled by a small hand wheel (3) and is not provided with an indicator. The aeroplane tends to turn to starboard when the hand wheel is rotated clockwise.

10. **Undercarriage control and Indicators (visual and audible)**

    (a) The undercarriage selector lever (75) moves in a gated quadrant, on the right hand side of the cockpit. An automatic cut-out in the control moves the selector lever into the gate when it has been pushed or pulled to the full extent of the quadrant.

Issued with A.L.No.19/F	A.P.1565B, Vol.I Sect.I

(b) To raise the undercarriage

The lever is pushed forward, but it must first be pulled back and then across to disengage it from the gate. When the undercarriage is raised and locked, the lever will spring into the forward gate.

(c) To lower the undercarriage

The lever is pulled back, but it must be pushed forward and then across to disengage it from the gate. When the undercarriage is lowered and locked, the lever will spring into the rear gate.

(d) Electrical visual indicator

The electrically operated visual indicator (22) has two semi-transparent windows on which the words UP on a red background and DOWN on a green background are lettered; the words are illuminated according to the position of the undercarriage. The switch for the DOWN circuit of the indicator is mounted on the inboard side of the throttle quadrant and is moved to the ON position by means of a striker on the throttle lever; this switch should be returned to the OFF position by hand when the aeroplane is left standing for any length of time. The UP circuit is not controlled by this switch.

(e) Mechanical position indicator

A rod that extends through the top surface of the main plane is fitted to each undercarriage unit. When the wheels are down the rods protrude through the top of the main planes and when they are up the top of the rods, which are painted red, are flush with the main plane surfaces.

(f) Warning horn

The push switch controlling the horn is mounted on the throttle quadrant and is operated by a striker on the throttle lever. The horn may be silenced, even though the wheels are retracted and the engine throttled back, by depressing the push button (9) on the side of the throttle quadrant. As soon as the throttle is again advanced beyond about one quarter of its travel the push-button is automatically released and the horn will sound again on its return.

F.S/3

Issued with A.L.No.19/F

11. Flap control

The split flaps have two positions only, up and fully down. They cannot therefore, be used to assist take-off. They are operated pneumatically and are controlled by a finger lever (25). A flap indicator was fitted only on early Spitfire I aeroplanes.

12. Undercarriage emergency operation

(a) A sealed high-pressure cylinder containing carbon-dioxide and connected to the undercarriage operating jacks is provided for use in the event of failure of the hydraulic system. The cylinder is mounted on the right hand side of the cockpit and the seal can be punctured by means of a red painted lever (76) beside it. The handle is marked EMERGENCY ONLY and provision is made for fitting a thin copper wire seal as a check against inadvertent use.

(b) If the hydraulic system fails, the pilot should ensure that the undercarriage selector lever is in the DOWN position (this is essential) and push the emergency lowering lever forward and downward. The angular travel of the emergency lever is about 100° for puncturing the seal of the cylinder and then releasing the piercing plunger; it must be pushed through this movement and allowed to swing downwards. NO attempt should be made to return it to its original position until the cylinder is being replaced.

13. Wheel brakes

The control lever (35) for the pneumatic brakes is fitted on the control column spade grip; differential control of the brakes is provided by a relay valve (43) connected to the rudder bar. A catch for retaining the brake lever in the on position for parking is fitted below the lever pivot. A triple pressure gauge (18), showing the air pressures in the pneumatic system cylinders and at each brake, is mounted on the left hand side of the instrument panel.

ENGINE CONTROLS

14. Throttle and mixture controls

The throttle and mixture levers (10 and 11) are fitted in a quadrant on the port side of the cockpit. A gate is provided for the throttle lever in the take-off position and an interlocking device between the levers prevents the engine from being run on an unsuitable mixture. Friction adjusters (8) for the controls are provided on the side of the quadrant.

Issued with A.L.No.19/F   A.P.1565B, Vol.I Sect.I

15. Automatic boost cut-out

   The automatic boost control may be cut out by pushing forward the small red painted lever (14) at the forward end of the throttle quadrant.

16. Airscrew controls

   The control lever (12) for the de Havilland 20° or Rotol 35° constant speed airscrew is on the throttle quadrant. The de Havilland 20° airscrew has a Positive Coarse Pitch position which is obtained in the extreme aft position of the control lever, when the airscrew blades are held at their maximum coarse pitch angles and the airscrew functions as a fixed airscrew.

17. Radiator flap control

   The flap at the outlet end of the radiator duct is operated by a lever (40) and ratchet on the left hand side of the cockpit. To open the flap, the lever should be pushed forward after releasing the ratchet by depressing the knob at the top of the lever. The normal minimum drag position of the flap lever for level flight is shown by a red triangle on the top of the map case fitted beside the lever. A notch beyond the normal position in the aft direction provides a position of the lever when the warm air is diverted through ducts into the main planes for heating the guns at high altitude.

18. Slow-running cut-out

   The control on the carburettor is operated by pulling the ring (74) on the right hand side of the instrument panel.

19. Fuel cock controls and contents gauges

   The fuel cock controls (38 and 39), one for each tank, are fitted at the bottom of the instrument panel. With the levers in the up position the cocks are open. Either tank can be isolated, if necessary. The fuel contents gauge (46) on the instrument panel indicates the contents of the lower tank, but only when the adjacent push button is pressed.

20. Fuel priming pump

   A hand-operated pump (44) for priming the engine is mounted below the right hand side of the instrument panel.

21. Ignition switches

   The ignition switches (17) are on the left hand bottom corner of the instrument panel.

F.S/4

Issued with A.L.No.19/F

22. **Cartridge starter**

   The starter push-button (47) at the bottom of the instrument panel operates the L.4 Coffman starter and the booster coil. The control (70) for reloading the breech is below the right-hand side of the instrument panel and is operated by slowly pulling on the finger ring and then releasing it.

23. **Hand starting**

   A starting handle is stowed behind the seat. A hole in the engine cowling panel on the starboard side gives access for connecting the handle to the hand starting gear.

24. **Engine instruments**

   The engine instruments are grouped on the right hand side of the instrument panel and comprise the following: engine-speed indicator (58), fuel pressure gauge (59), boost gauge (61), oil pressure gauge (69), oil inlet temperature gauge (67), radiator outlet temperature gauge (63) and fuel contents gauge (46).

   COCKPIT ACCOMMODATION AND EQUIPMENT

25. **Pilot's seat control**

   The seat is adjustable for height by means of a lever on the right hand side of the seat.

26. **Safety harness release**

   In order that the pilot may lean forward without unfastening his harness, a release catch (73) is fitted to the right of the seat.

27. **Cockpit door**

   To facilitate entry to the cockpit a portion of the coaming on the port side is hinged. The door catches are released by means of a handle at the forward end. Two position catches are incorporated to allow the door to be partly opened before taking off or landing in order to prevent the hood from sliding shut in the event of a mishap.

28. **Hood locking control**

   The sliding hood is provided with spring catches for holding it either open or shut; the catches are released by two finger levers at the forward end of the hood. From outside, with the hood closed, the catches can be released by depressing a small knob at the top of the windscreen. Provision is made on the door to prevent the hood from sliding shut if the aeroplane over-turns on landing.

Issued with A.L.No.19/F

29. Direct vision panel -

A small knock-out panel is provided on the right hand side of the hood for use in the event of the windscreen becoming obscured.

30. Cockpit lighting -

A floodlight (62) is fitted on each side of the cockpit and is dimmed by a switch (34) immediately below the instrument panel.

31. Cockpit heating and ventilation -

A small adjustable flap on the starboard coaming above the instrument panel is provided for ventilation of the cockpit. The flap is opened by turning a knurled nut (57) underneath the flap.

32. Oxygen -

A standard regulator unit (23) is fitted on the left hand side of the instrument panel and a bayonet socket (65) is on the right hand side of the cockpit. A separate cock is provided in addition to the regulator.

33. Mirror -

A mirror providing a rearward view is fitted at the top of the windscreen.

34. Map cases -

A metal case (6) for a writing pad and another (2) for maps, books etc. are fitted on the left hand side of the cockpit. Stowage (71) for a height-and-airspeed computor is provided below the wireless remote contactor.

OPERATIONAL EQUIPMENT AND CONTROLS

35.(a) Guns and cannon -

The eight machine guns on the Spitfire IIA are fired pneumatically by a push-button on the control column spade grip. The compressed air supply is taken from the same source as the brake supply, the available pressure being shown by the gauge (18). The push-button is surrounded by a milled sleeve which can be rotated by a quarter of a turn to a safe position in which it prevents operation of the button. The SAFE and FIRE positions are engraved on the sleeve and can also be identified by touch as the sleeve has an indentation which is at the bottom when the sleeve is in the SAFE position and is at the side when the sleeve is turned to the FIRE position.

Issued with A.L.No.19/F

(b) The guns and cannon on the Spitfire IIB are fired pneumatically by a triple push-button on the control column spade grip. A milled finger lever extending from the bottom of the push button casing provides the means of locking the button in the SAFE position, SAFE and FIRE being engraved on the adjacent casing. When the lever is in the FIRE position a pip extends also from the top of the casing enabling the pilot to ascertain by feel the setting of the push button.

(c) To prevent accidental firing of the cannon on the ground, a safety valve is fitted in the firing system. This is mounted below the undercarriage control unit and is coupled to the undercarriage locking pin cable in such a way that the cannon firing system is inoperative when the wheels are locked down. For practice firing at the butts however, a finger lever on the safety valve can be operated to allow the use of the firing system.

(d) The cannons are cocked pneumatically by a cocking valve mounted on the right-hand side of the cockpit.

36. Reflector gun sight

a) For sighting the guns and cannon a reflector gun sight is mounted on a bracket (53) above the instrument panel. A main switch (50) and dimmer switch (51) are fitted below the mounting bracket. The dimmer switch has three positions marked OFF, NIGHT and DAY. Three spare lamps for the sight are stowed in holders (60) on the right hand side of the cockpit.

b) When the sight is used during the day the dimmer switch should be in the DAY position in order to give full illumination, and if the background of the target is very bright, a sun-screen (54) can be slid behind the windscreen by pulling on the ring (52) at the top of the instrument panel. For night use the dimmer switch should be in the NIGHT position; in this position a low-wattage lamp is brought into circuit and the light can be varied by rotating the switch knob.

Issued with A.L. No. 19/F   A.P.1565B, Vol.I Sect.I

37. **Camera**

   (a) A G.42B cine-camera is fitted in the leading edge of the port plane, near the root end and is operated by the cannon-firing button on the control column spade grip, a succession of exposures being made during the whole time the button is depressed, provided the selector switch (5) on the left-hand side of the cockpit is ON.

   (b) A footage indicator and an aperture switch are mounted on the wedge plate above the throttle lever. The switch enables either of two camera apertures to be selected, the smaller aperture being used for sunny weather. A stowage clip is provided to receive the electrical cable (13) when the indicator and switch are not fitted.

   NAVIGATIONAL, SIGNALLING AND LIGHTING EQUIPMENT

38. **Wireless**

   (a) The aeroplane is equipped with a combined transmitter-receiver, either type T.R.9D or T.R.1133, and an R.3002 set.

   (b) With the T.R.9D installation a type C mechanical controller (19) is fitted on the port side of the cockpit above the throttle lever and a remote contactor (66) and contactor master switch are fitted on the right hand side of the cockpit. The master contactor is mounted behind the pilot's headrest and a switch controlling the heating element is fitted on the forward bracket of the mounting. The heating element should always be switched OFF when the pilot leaves the aeroplane. The microphone/telephone socket is fitted on the right hand side of the pilot's seat.

   (c) With the T.R.1133 installation the contactor gear and microphone/telephone socket are as for the T.R.9D installation, but the type C mechanical controller is replaced by a push-button electrical control unit.

39. **Navigation and identification lamps**

   (a) The switch (24) controlling the navigation lamps is on the instrument panel.

F.S/6

Issued with A.L. No. 19/F

   (b) The upward and downward identification lamps are controlled from the signalling switchbox (64) on the right hand side of the cockpit. This switchbox has a switch for each lamp and a morsing key, and provides for steady illumination or morse signalling from each lamp or both. The switch lever has three positions: MORSE, OFF and STEADY.

   (c) The spring pressure on the morsing key can be adjusted by turning the small ring at the top left hand corner of the switchbox, adjustment being maintained by a latch engaging one of a number of notches in the ring. The range of movement of the key can be adjusted by opening the cover and adjusting the screw and locknut at the centre of the cover.

40. Landing lamps

The landing lamps, one on each side of the aeroplane, are housed in the undersurface of the main plane. They are lowered and raised by a finger lever (36) below the instrument panel. Each lamp has an independent electrical circuit and is controlled by a switch (16) above the pneumatic control lever (36) with the switch in the central position both lamps are off; when the switch is moved to the left or to the right, the port or the starboard lamp respectively, is illuminated. A lever (15) is provided to control the dipping of both landing lamps. On pulling up the lever the beam is dipped.

41. Signal discharger

A straight pull of the toggle control on the left hand side of the cockpit fires one of the cartridges out of the top of the fuselage, aft of the cockpit.

DE-ICING EQUIPMENT

42. Windscreen de-icing

   (a) A tank containing the de-icing solution is mounted on the left-hand side of the cockpit directly above the bottom longeron. A cock is mounted above the tank, and a pump and a needle valve to control the flow of the liquid are mounted below the undercarriage emergency lowering control. Liquid is pumped from the tank to a spray at the base of the windscreen, from which it is sprayed upwards over the front panel of the screen.

Issued with A.L. No. 19/F　　　　　　　　A.P.1565B, Vol.I Sect.I

(b) The flow of liquid is governed by the needle valve, after turning ON the cock and pushing down the pump plunger to its full extent. The plunger will return to the extended position on its own, and if required it can be pushed down again. When de-icing is no longer required the cock should be turned to the OFF position.

43.   Pressure head heater switch

The heating element in the pressure head is controlled by a switch (4) below the trimming tab handwheels. It should be switched off on landing in order to conserve the battery.

EMERGENCY EQUIPMENT

44.   Hood jettisoning

The hood may be jettisoned in an emergency by pulling the lever mounted inside the top of the hood in a forward and downward movement, and pushing the lower edge of the hood outboard with the elbows. On aeroplanes not fitted with a jettison type hood, a crowbar is provided to assist in jettisoning the hood.

45.   Forced landing flare

A forced landing flare is carried in a tube fixed inside the fuselage. The flare is released by means of a ring grip (1) on the left of the pilot's seat.

46.   First aid

The first aid outfit is stowed aft of the wireless equipment and is accessible through a hinged panel on the port side of the fuselage.

Key to fig.1

Port side of cockpit

1. Flare release control
2. Map storage box
3. Rudder trimming tab control
4. Pressure head heating switch
5. Camera-gun master switch
6. Writing pad container
7. Elevator trimming tab control
8. Throttle and mixture friction adjusters
9. Push switch for silencing warning horn
10. Throttle lever
11. Mixture lever
12. Airscrew control lever
13. Connection for cine-camera footage indicator
14. Boost cut-out control
15. Landing lamp dipping lever
16. Landing lamps switch
17. Main magneto switches
18. Brake triple pressure gauge
19. Wireless remote controller
20. Clock
21. Elevator trimming tabs position indicator
22. Undercarriage position indicator
23. Oxygen regulator
24. Navigation lamps switch
25. Flaps control

27. Instrument-flying panel
28. Airspeed indicator
29. Artificial horizon
30. Altimeter
31. Direction indicator
32. Setting knob for (31)
33. Compass deviation card holder
34. Cockpit lamp dimmer switches
35. Brake lever
36. Landing lamp lowering control
37. Control column
38. Fuel cock lever (top tank)
39. Fuel cock lever (bottom tank)
40. Radiator flap control lever
41. Rudder pedals
42. Rudder pedal leg reach adjusters

A.P.1565B, VOL.I, SECT.1

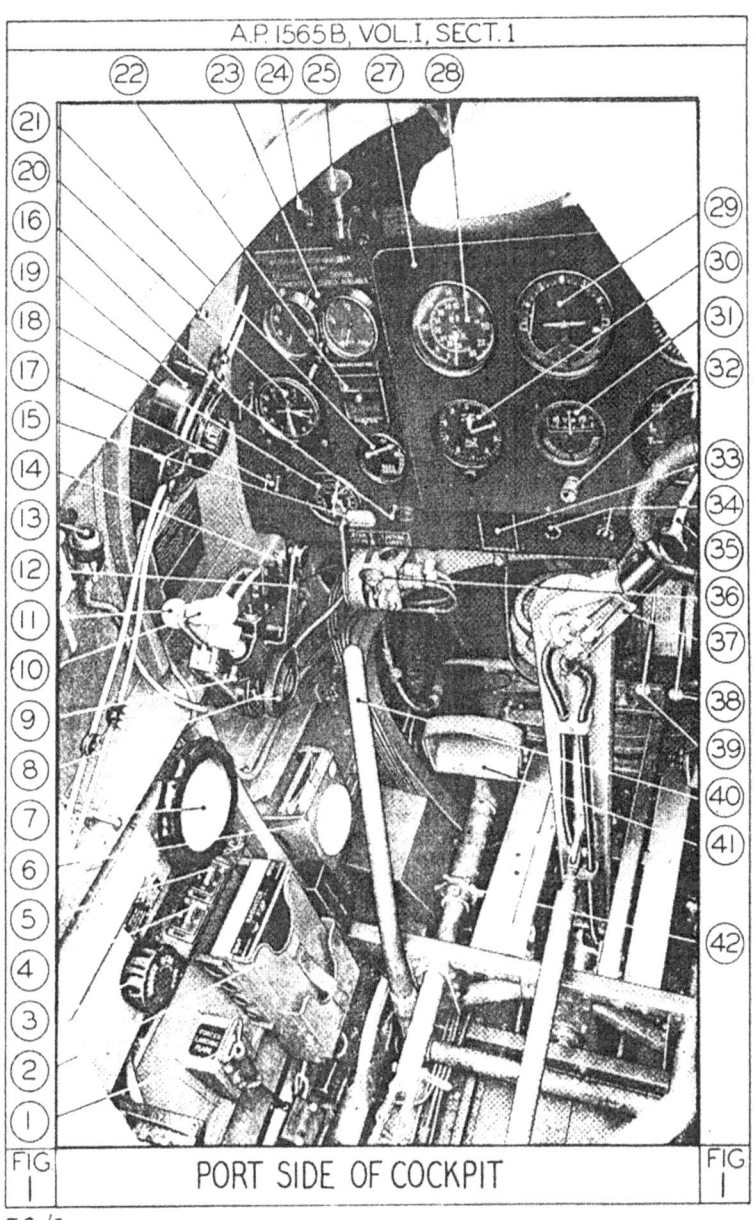

PORT SIDE OF COCKPIT

FIG 1

Key to fig. 2

Starboard side of cockpit

29.	Artificial horizon
31.	Direction indicator
34.	Cockpit lamp dimmer switch
38.	Fuel cock lever (top tank)
39.	Fuel cock lever (bottom tank)
43.	Brake relay valve
44.	Priming pump
45.	Compass
46.	Fuel contents gauge
47.	Engine starting pushbutton
48.	Turning indicator
49.	Rate of climb indicator
50.	Reflector sight main switch
51.	Reflector sight lamp dimmer switch
52.	Lifting ring for dimming screen
53.	Reflector gun sight mounting
54.	Dimming screen
55.	Ammeter
56.	Generator switch
57.	Ventilator control
58.	Engine speed indicator
59.	Fuel pressure gauge
60.	Spare filaments for reflector sight
61.	Boost gauge
62.	Cockpit lamp
63.	Radiator temperature gauge
64.	Signalling switch box
65.	Oxygen socket
66.	Wireless remote contactor mounting and switch
67.	Oil temperature gauge
68.	Engine data plate
69.	Oil pressure gauge
70.	Cartridge starter reloading control
71.	Height and airspeed computor stowage
72.	Control locking lug
73.	Harness release
74.	Slow-running cut-out control
75.	Undercarriage control lever
76.	Undercarriage emergency lowering lever
77.	Control locking lug

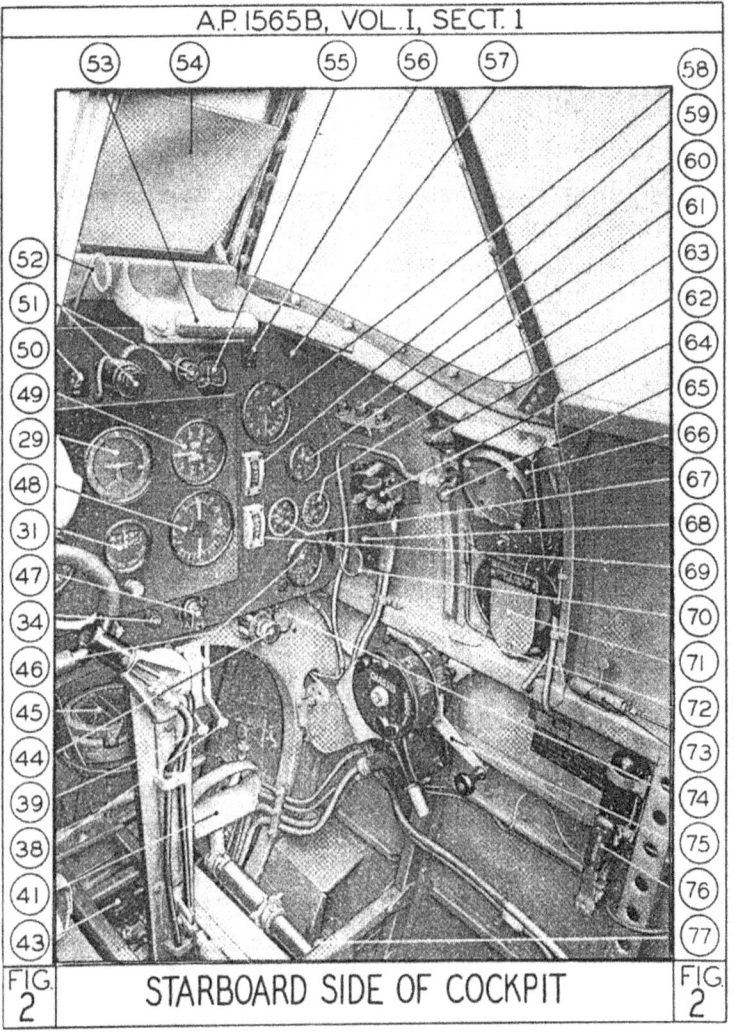

STARBOARD SIDE OF COCKPIT

Fig. 2

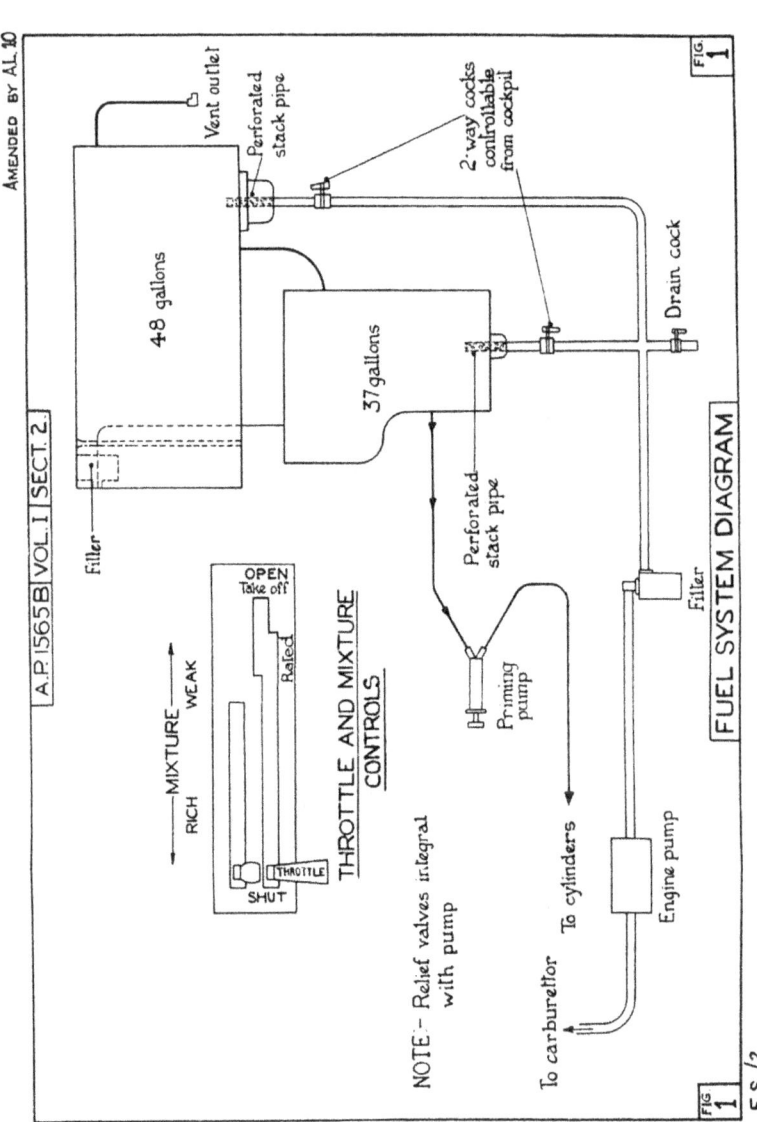

Revised December 1941. AIR PUBLICATION 1565B.
Issued with A.L.No.19/F Volume I and
Pilot's Notes.

SECTION I

PILOT'S CONTROLS AND EQUIPMENT.

INTRODUCTION

1. The Spitfire IIA and IIB are single seat, low wing monoplane fighters each fitted with a Merlin XII engine and a de Havilland 20° (P.C.P.) or Rotol 35° constant speed airscrew.

MAIN SERVICES

2. Fuel system.- Fuel is carried in two tanks mounted one above the other (the lower one is self-sealing) forward of the cockpit and is delivered by an engine driven pump. The tank capacities are as follows:

        Top tank: 48 gallons
        Bottom tank: 37 gallons

The top tank feeds into the lower tank, and the fuel cock controls (38 and 39), one for each tank, are fitted below the instrument panel.

3. Oil system.- Oil is supplied by a tank of 5.8 gallons capacity fitted below the engine mounting, and two oil coolers in tandem are fitted in the underside of the port plane.

4. Hydraulic system.- An engine-driven hydraulic pump supplies the power for operating the undercarriage.

5. Pneumatic system.- An engine-driven air compressor feeds two storage cylinders for operation of the flaps, brakes, guns and landing lamps. The cylinders are connected in series, each holding air at 200 lb/sq.in pressure.

6. Electrical system.- A 12 Volt generator, controlled by a switch (56) above the instrument panel, supplies an accumulator which in turn supplies the whole of the electrical installation. There is a voltmeter (55) on the left of the switch.

F.S/2

Issued with A.L. No.19/F.

AEROPLANE CONTROLS.

7. (a) **Primary flying controls and locking devices.**- The control column (37) is of the spade-grip pattern and incorporates the brake lever and gun and cannon firing control. The rudder pedals (41) have two positions for the feet and are adjustable for leg reach by rotation of star wheels (42) on the sliding tubes.

   (b) Control locking struts are stowed on the right hand side of the cockpit, behind the seat. To lock the control column, the longer strut should be clamped to the control column handle at one end and the other end inserted in a key-hole slot in the right hand side of the seat. The fixed pin on the free end of the arm attached to this strut at the control column end should then be inserted in a lug (72) on the starboard datum longeron, thus forming a rigid triangle between the column, the seat and the longeron.

   (c) To lock the rudder pedals, a short bar with a pin at each end is attached to the other struts by a cable. The longer of the two pins should be inserted in a hole in the starboard star wheel bearing and the shorter in an eyebolt (77) on the fuselage frame directly below the front edge of the seat. The controls should be locked with the seat in its highest position.

8. **Flying instruments.**- A standard blind flying instrument panel is incorporated in the main panel. The instruments comprise airspeed indicator (28), altimeter (30), directional gyro (31), artificial horizon (29), rate of climb and descent indicator (49), and turn and bank indicator (48).

9. **Trimming tabs.**- The elevator trimming tabs are controlled by a hand wheel (7) on the left hand side of the cockpit, the indicator (21) being on the instrument panel. The rudder trimming tab is controlled by a small hand wheel (3) and is not provided with an indicator. The aeroplane tends to turn to starboard when the handwheel is rotated clockwise.

10. (a) **Undercarriage control and Indicators (visual and audible)** The undercarriage selector lever (75) moves in a gated quadrant, on the right hand side of the cockpit. An automatic cut-out in the control moves the selector lever into the gate when it has been pushed or pulled to the full extent of the quadrant.

Issued with A.L.No.19/F.   A.P.1565B, Vol.I Sect.I.

(b) To raise the undercarriage the lever is pushed forward, but it must first be pulled back and then across to disengage it from the gate. When the undercarriage is raised and locked, the lever will spring into the forward gate.

(c) To lower the undercarriage the lever is pulled back, but it must be pushed forward and then across to disengage it from the gate. When the undercarriage is lowered and locked, the lever will spring into the rear gate.

(d) Electrical visual indicator.- The electrically operated visual indicator (22) has two semi-transparent windows on which the words UP on a red background and DOWN on a green background are lettered; the words are illuminated according to the position of the undercarriage. The switch for the DOWN circuit of the indicator is mounted on the inboard side of the throttle quadrant and is moved to the ON position by means of a striker on the throttle lever; this switch should be returned to the OFF position by hand when the aeroplane is left standing for any length of time. The UP circuit is not controlled by this switch.

(e) Mechanical position indicator.- A rod that extends through the top surface of the main plane is fitted to each undercarriage unit. When the wheels are down the rods protrude through the top of the main planes and when they are up the top of the rods, which are painted red, are flush with the main plane surfaces.

(f) Warning horn.- The push switch controlling the horn is mounted on the throttle quadrant and is operated by a striker on the throttle lever. The horn may be silenced, even though the wheels are retracted and the engine throttled back, by depressing the push button (9) on the side of the throttle quadrant. As soon as the throttle is again advanced beyond about one quarter of its travel the push - button is automatically released and the horn will sound again on its return.

F.S/3.

Issued with A.L. No.19/F.

11. **Flap control.-** The split flaps have two positions only, up and fully down. They cannot therefore, be used to assist take-off. They are operated pneumatically and are controlled by a finger lever (25). A flap indicator was fitted only on early Spitfire I aeroplanes.

12. (a) **Undercarriage emergency operation.-** A sealed high-pressure cylinder containing carbon-dioxide and connected to the undercarriage operating jacks is provided for use in the event of failure of the hydraulic system. The cylinder is mounted on the right hand side of the cockpit and the seal can be punctured by means of a red painted lever (76) beside it. The handle is marked EMERGENCY ONLY and provision is made for fitting a thin copper wire seal as a check against inadvertent use.

   (b) If the hydraulic system fails, the pilot should ensure that the undercarriage selector lever is in the DOWN position (this is essential) and push the emergency lowering lever forward and downward. The angular travel of the emergency lever is about 100° for puncturing the seal of the cylinder and then releasing the piercing plunger; it must be pushed through this movement and allowed to swing downwards. NO attempt should be made to return it to its original position until the cylinder is being replaced.

13. **Wheel brakes.-** The control lever (35) for the pneumatic brakes is fitted on the control column spade grip; differential control of the brakes is provided by a relay valve (43) connected to the rudder bar. A catch for retaining the brake lever in the on position for parking is fitted below the lever pivot. A triple pressure gauge (18), showing the air pressures in the pneumatic system cylinders and at each brake, is mounted on the left hand side of the instrument panel.

ENGINE CONTROLS.

14. **Throttle and mixture controls.-** The throttle and mixture levers (10 and 11) are fitted in a quadrant on the port side of the cockpit. A gate is provided for the throttle lever in the take-off position and an interlocking device between the levers prevents the engine from being run on an unsuitable mixture. Friction adjusters (8) for the controls are provided on the side of the quadrant.

Issued with A.L.No.19/F   A.P.1565B, Vol.I Sect.I.

15. **Automatic boost cut-out.-** The automatic boost control may be cut out by pushing forward the small red painted lever (14) at the forward end of the throttle quadrant.

16. **Airscrew controls.-** The control lever (12) for the de Havilland 20° or Rotol 35° constant speed airscrew is on the throttle quadrant. The de Havilland 20° airscrew has a Positive Coarse Pitch position which is obtained in the extreme aft position of the control lever, when the airscrew blades are held at their maximum coarse pitch angles and the airscrew functions as a fixed airscrew.

17. **Radiator flap control.-** The flap at the outlet end of the radiator duct is operated by a lever (40) and ratchet on the left hand side of the cockpit. To open the flap, the lever should be pushed forward after releasing the ratchet by depressing the knob at the top of the lever. The normal minimum drag position of the flap lever for level flight is shown by a red triangle on the top of the map case fitted beside the lever. A notch beyond the normal position in the aft direction provides a position of the lever when the warm air is diverted through ducts into the main planes for heating the guns at high altitude.

18. **Slow-running cut-out.-** The control on the carburettor is operated by pulling the ring (74) on the right hand side of the instrument panel.

19. **Fuel cock controls and contents gauges.-** The fuel cock controls (38 and 39), one for each tank, are fitted at the bottom of the instrument panel. With the levers in the up position the cocks are open. Either tank can be isolated, if necessary. The fuel contents gauge (46) on the instrument panel indicates the contents of the lower tank, but only when the adjacent push button is pressed.

20. **Fuel priming pump.-** A hand-operated pump (44) for priming the engine is mounted below the right hand side of the instrument panel.

21. **Ignition switches.-** The ignition switches (17) are on the left hand bottom corner of the instrument panel.

F.S/4.

Issued with A.L.No.19/F

22. **Cartridge starter.-** The starter push-button (47) at the bottom of the instrument panel operates the L.4 Coffman starter and the booster coil. The control (70) for reloading the breech is below the right-hand side of the instrument panel and is operated by slowly pulling on the finger ring and then releasing it.

23. **Hand starting.-** A starting handle is stowed behind the seat. A hole in the engine cowling panel on the starboard side gives access for connecting the handle to the hand starting gear.

24. **Engine instruments.-** The engine instruments are grouped on the right hand side of the instrument panel and comprise the following: engine-speed indicator (58), fuel pressure gauge (59), boost gauge (61), oil pressure gauge (69), oil inlet temperature gauge (67), radiator outlet temperature gauge (63) and fuel contents gauge (46).

COCKPIT ACCOMMODATION AND EQUIPMENT

25. **Pilot's seat control.-** The seat is adjustable for height by means of a lever on the right hand side of the seat.

26. **Safety harness release.-** In order that the pilot may lean forward without unfastening his harness, a release catch (73) is fitted to the right of the seat.

27. **Cockpit door.-** To facilitate entry to the cockpit a portion of the coaming on the port side is hinged. The door catches are released by means of a handle at the forward end. Two position catches are incorporated to allow the door to be partly opened before taking off or landing in order to prevent the hood from sliding shut in the event of a mishap.

28. **Hood locking control.-** The sliding hood is provided with spring catches for holding it either open or shut; the catches are released by two finger levers at the forward end of the hood. From outside, with the hood closed, the catches can be released by depressing a small knob at the top of the windscreen. Provision is made on the door to prevent the hood from sliding shut if the aeroplane over-turns on landing.

Issued with A.L.No.19/F A.P.1565B, Vol.I Sect.I.

29. **Direct vision panel.**- A small knock-out panel is provided on the right hand side of the hood for use in the event of the windscreen becoming obscured.

30. **Cockpit lighting.**- A floodlight (62) is fitted on each side of the cockpit and is dimmed by a switch (34) immediately below the instrument panel.

31. **Cockpit heating and ventilation.**- A small adjustable flap on the starboard coaming above the instrument panel is provided for ventilation of the cockpit. The flap is opened by turning a knurled nut (57) underneath the flap.

32. **Oxygen.**- A standard regulator unit (23) is fitted on the left hand side of the instrument panel and a bayonet socket (65) is on the right hand side of the cockpit. A separate cock is provided in addition to the regulator.

33. **Mirror.**- A mirror providing a rearward view is fitted at the top of the windscreen.

34. **Map cases.**- A metal case (6) for a writing pad and another (2) for maps, books etc. are fitted on the left hand side of the cockpit. Stowage (71) for a height-and-airspeed computor is provided below the wireless remote contactor.

OPERATIONAL EQUIPMENT AND CONTROLS

35. (a) **Guns and cannon.**- The eight machine guns on the Spitfire IIA are fired pneumatically by a push-button on the control column spade grip. The compressed air supply is taken from the same source as the brake supply, the available pressure being shown by the gauge (18). The push-button is surrounded by a milled sleeve which can be rotated by a quarter of a turn to a safe position in which it prevents operation of the button. The SAFE and FIRE positions are engraved on the sleeve and can also be identified by touch as the sleeve has an indentation which is at the bottom when the sleeve is in the SAFE position and is at the side when the sleeve is turned to the FIRE position.

F.S/5.

Issued with A.L.No.19/F

- (b) The guns and cannon on the Spitfire IIB are fired pneumatically by a triple push-button on the control column spade grip. A milled finger lever extending from the bottom of the push button casing provides the means of locking the button in the SAFE position, SAFE and FIRE being engraved on the adjacent casing. When the lever is in the FIRE position a pip extends also from the top of the casing enabling the pilot to ascertain by feel the setting of the push button.

- (c) To prevent accidental firing of the cannon on the ground, a safety valve is fitted in the firing system. This is mounted below the undercarriage control unit and is coupled to the undercarriage locking pin cable in such a way that the cannon firing system is inoperative when the wheels are locked down. For practice firing at the butts however, a finger lever on the safety valve can be operated to allow the use of the firing system.

- (d) The cannon are cocked pneumatically by a cocking valve mounted on the right-hand side of the cockpit.

36. (a) Reflector gun sight.- For sighting the guns and cannon a reflector gun sight is mounted on a bracket (53) above the instrument panel. A main switch (50) and dimmer switch (51) are fitted below the mounting bracket. The dimmer switch has three positions marked OFF, NIGHT and DAY. Three spare lamps for the sight are stowed in holders (60) on the right hand side of the cockpit.

- (b) When the sight is used during the day the dimmer switch should be in the DAY position in order to give full illumination, and if the background of the target is very bright, a sun-screen (54) can be slid behind the windscreen by pulling on the ring (52) at the top of the instrument panel. For night use the dimmer switch should be in the NIGHT position; in this position a low-wattage lamp is brought into circuit and the light can be varied by rotating the switch knob.

Issued with A.L.No.19/F A.P.1565B, Vol.I Sect.I.

37. (a) **Camera.-** A G.42B cine-camera is fitted in the leading edge of the port plane, near the root end and is operated by the cannon-firing button on the control column spade grip, a succession of exposures being made during the whole time the button is depressed, provided the selector switch (5) on the left-hand side of the cockpit is ON.

   (b) A footage indicator and an aperture switch are mounted on the wedge plate above the throttle lever The switch enables either of two camera apertures to be selected, the smaller aperture being used for sunny weather. A stowage clip is provided to receive the electrical cable (13) when the indicator and switch are not fitted.

NAVIGATIONAL, SIGNALLING AND LIGHTING EQUIPMENT.

38. (a) **Wireless.-** The aeroplane is equipped with a combined transmitter-receiver, either type T.R.9D or T.R.1133, and an R.3002 set.

   (b) With the T.R.9D installation a type C mechanical controller (19) is fitted on the port side of the cockpit above the throttle lever and a remote contactor (66) and contactor master switch are fitted on the right hand side of the cockpit. The master contactor is mounted behind the pilot's headrest and a switch controlling the heating element is fitted on the forward bracket of the mounting. The heating element should always be switched OFF when the pilot leaves the aeroplane. The microphone/telephone socket is fitted on the right hand side of the pilot's seat.

   (c) With the T.R.1133 installation the contactor gear and microphone/telephone socket are as for the T.R.9D installation, but the type C mechanical controller is replaced by a push-button electrical control unit.

39. (a) **Navigation and identification lamps.-** The switch (24) controlling the navigation lamps is on the instrument panel.

F.S/6

Issued with A.L.No.19/F

(b) The upward and downward identification lamps are controlled from the signalling switchbox (64) on the right hand side of the cockpit. This switchbox has a switch for each lamp and a morsing key, and provides for steady illumination or morse signalling from each lamp or both. The switch lever has three positions: MORSE, OFF and STEADY.

(c) The spring pressure on the morsing key can be adjusted by turning the small ring at the top left hand corner of the switchbox, adjustment being maintained by a latch engaging one of a number of notches in the ring. The range of movement of the key can be adjusted by opening the cover and adjusting the screw and locknut at the centre of the cover.

40. Landing lamps.- The landing lamps, one on each side of the aeroplane, are housed in the undersurface of the main plane. They are lowered and raised by a finger lever (36) below the instrument panel. Each lamp has an independent electrical circuit and is controlled by a switch (16) above the pneumatic control lever (36) with the switch in the central position both lamps are off; when the switch is moved to the left or to the right, the port or the starboard lamp respectively, is illuminated. A lever (15) is provided to control the dipping of both landing lamps. On pulling up the lever the beam is dipped.

41. Signal discharger.- A straight pull of the toggle control on the left hand side of the cockpit fires one of the cartridges out of the top of the fuselage, aft of the cockpit.

DE-ICING EQUIPMENT.

42.(a) Windscreen de-icing.- A tank containing the de-icing solution is mounted on the left-hand side of the cockpit directly above the bottom longeron. A cock is mounted above the tank, and a pump and a needle valve to control the flow of the liquid are mounted below the undercarriage emergency lowering control. Liquid is pumped from the tank to a spray at the base of the windscreen, from which it is sprayed upwards over the front panel of the screen.

Issued with A.L.No.19/F   A.P.1565B, Vol.I Sect.I.

(b) The flow of liquid is governed by the needle valve, after turning ON the cock and pushing down the pump plunger to its full extent. The plunger will return to the extended position on its own, and if required it can be pushed down again. When de-icing is no longer required the cock should be turned to the OFF position.

43. Pressure head heater switch.- The heating element in the pressure head is controlled by a switch (4) below the trimming tab handwheels. It should be switched off on landing in order to conserve the battery.

EMERGENCY EQUIPMENT

44. Hood jettisoning.- The hood may be jettisoned in an emergency by pulling the lever mounted inside the top of the hood in a forward and downward movement, and pushing the lower edge of the hood outboard with the elbows. On aeroplanes not fitted with a jettison type hood, a crowbar is provided to assist in jettisoning the hood.

45. Forced landing flare.- A forced landing flare is carried in a tube fixed inside the fuselage. The flare is released by means of a ring grip (1) on the left of the pilot's seat.

46. First aid.- The first aid outfit is stowed aft of the wireless equipment and is accessible through a hinged panel on the port side of the fuselage.

F.8/7

Key to fig. 1

Port side of cockpit

1. Flare release control
2. Map stowage box
3. Rudder trimming tab control
4. Pressure head heating switch
5. Camera-gun master switch
6. Writing pad container
7. Elevator trimming tab control
8. Throttle and mixture friction adjusters
9. Push switch for silencing warning horn
10. Throttle lever
11. Mixture lever
12. Airscrew control lever
13. Connection for cine-camera footage indicator
14. Boost cut-out control
15. Landing lamp dipping lever
16. Landing lamps switch
17. Main magneto switches
18. Brake triple pressure gauge
19. Wireless remote controller
20. Clock
21. Elevator trimming tabs position indicator
22. Undercarriage position indicator
23. Oxygen regulator
24. Navigation lamps switch
25. Flaps control

27. Instrument-flying panel
28. Airspeed indicator
29. Artificial horizon
30. Altimeter
31. Direction indicator
32. Setting knob for (31)
33. Compass deviation card holder
34. Cockpit lamp dimmer switches
35. Brake lever
36. Landing lamp lowering control
37. Control column
38. Fuel cock lever (top tank)
39. Fuel cock lever (bottom tank)
40. Radiator flap control lever
41. Rudder pedals
42. Rudder pedal leg reach adjusters

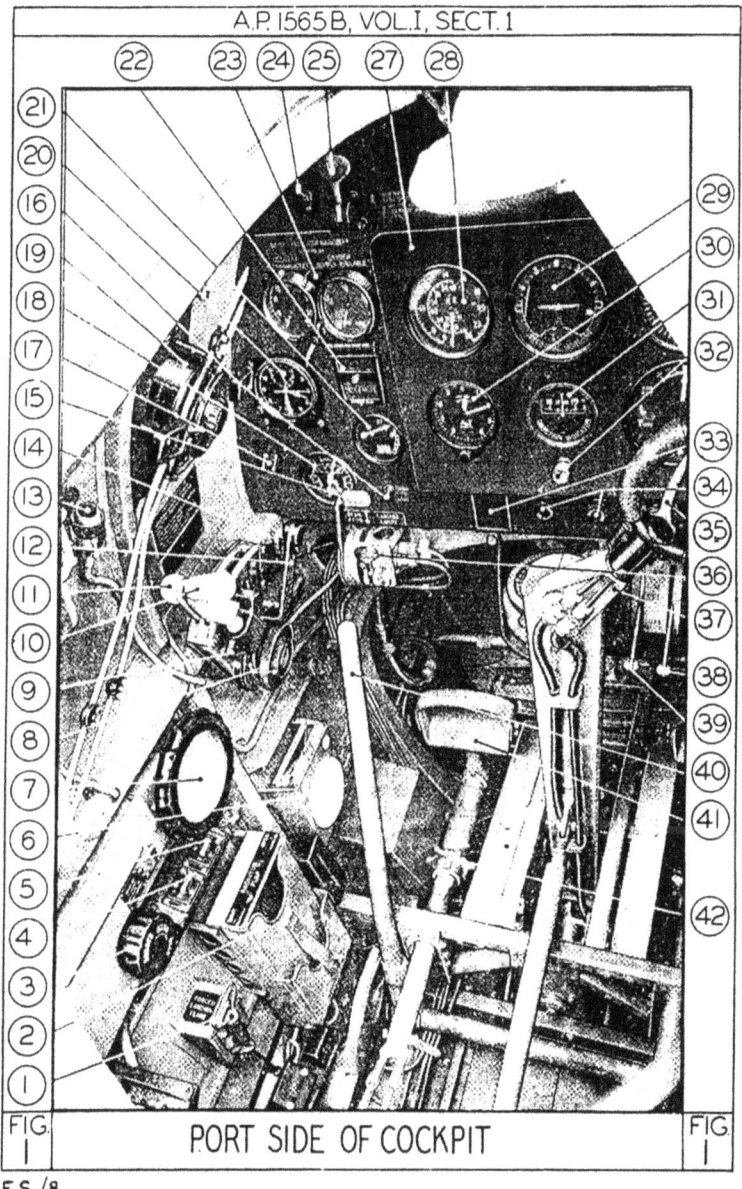

PORT SIDE OF COCKPIT

Key to fig.2

Starboard side of cockpit

29. Artificial horizon
31. Direction indicator
34. Cockpit lamp dimmer switch
38. Fuel cock lever (top tank)
39. Fuel cock lever (bottom tank)
43. Brake relay valve
44. Priming pump
45. Compass
46. Fuel contents gauge
47. Engine starting pushbutton
48. Turning indicator
49. Rate of climb indicator
50. Reflector sight main switch
51. Reflector sight lamp dimmer switch
52. Lifting ring for dimming screen
53. Reflector gun sight mounting
54. Dimming screen
55. Ammeter
56. Generator switch
57. Ventilator control
58. Engine speed indicator
59. Fuel pressure gauge
60. Spare filaments for reflector sight
61. Boost gauge
62. Cockpit lamp
63. Radiator temperature gauge
64. Signalling switch box
65. Oxygen socket
66. Wireless remote contactor mounting and switch
67. Oil temperature gauge
68. Engine data plate
69. Oil pressure gauge
70. Cartridge starter reloading control
71. Height and airspeed computor stowage
72. Control locking lug
73. Harness release
74. Slow-running cut-out control
75. Undercarriage control lever
76. Undercarriage emergency lowering lever
77. Control locking lug

STARBOARD SIDE OF COCKPIT

FIG. 2

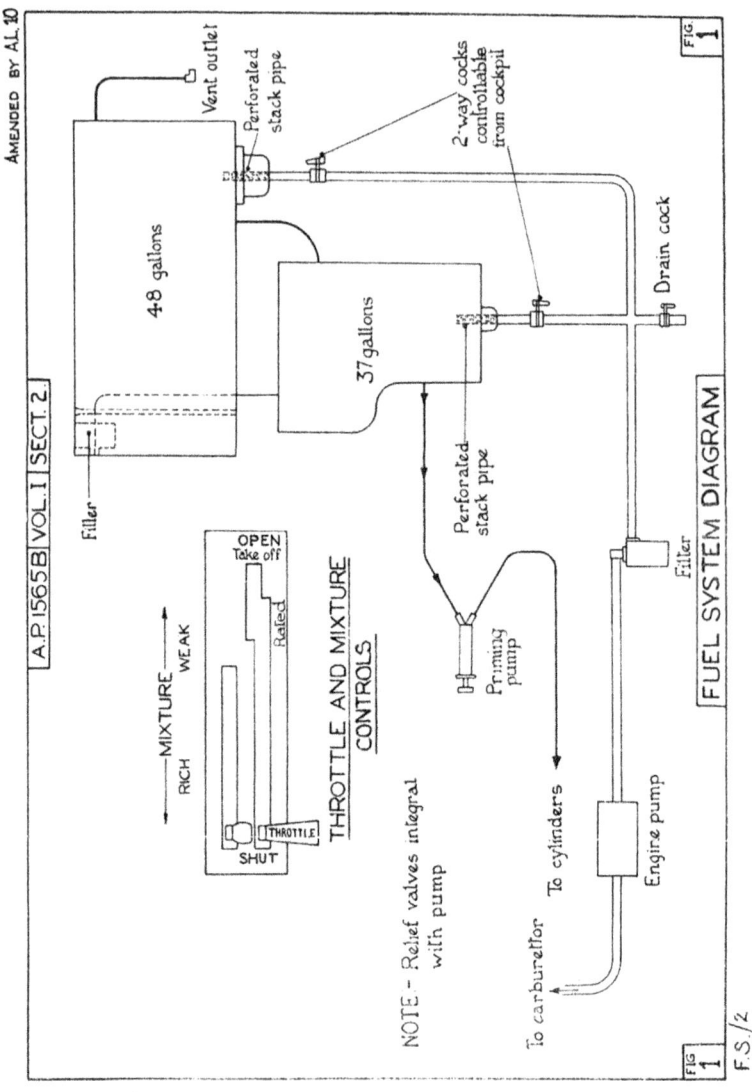

Amended in Vol. I by A.L.31
and in P.N. by A.L./L.

AIR PUBLICATION 1565B
Volume I and Pilot's Notes

SECTION 2

HANDLING AND FLYING NOTES FOR PILOT

1. ENGINE DATA: MERLIN XII

    (i) **Fuel:** 100 octane (the reduced limitations for use with 87 octane fuel are shown in brackets)

    (ii) **Oil:** See A.P.1464/C.37.

    (iii) **Engine limitations:**

	R.p.m.	Boost lb/sq.in.	Temp. °C Clnt.	Oil
MAX. TAKE-OFF TO 1,000 FEET	3,000	+12½(+7)	–	–
MAX. CLIMBING 1 HR. LIMIT	2,850	+ 9 (+7)	125	90
MAX. RICH CONTINUOUS	2,650	+ 7 (+5)	105*	90
MAX. WEAK CONTINUOUS	2,650	+ 4 (+2½)	105*	90
COMBAT 5 MINS. LIMIT	3,000	+12 (+7)	135	105

    * 115°C permitted for short periods if necessary

    Note: +12 lb/sq.in. combat boost is obtained by operating the boost control cut-out and is effective up to about 10,500 feet.

    OIL PRESSURE: MINM. IN FLIGHT: 30 lb/sq.in.

    MINM. TEMP. FOR TAKE-OFF: OIL: 15°C
    COOLANT: 60°C

    FUEL PRESSURE: NORMAL: 2½-3 lb/sq.in.

F.S/3

(iv) <u>Other limitations</u>:

    Diving: Maximum r.p.m. : 3,600
                       3,000 r.p.m. may be exceeded only
                       for 20 seconds, with the throttle
                       not less than one-third open.

(v) <u>Combat concession</u>:

    3,000 r.p.m. may be used above 20,000 feet for periods
    not exceeding 30 minutes.

2.   FLYING LIMITATIONS

(i) <u>Maximum speeds (m.p.h. I.A.S.)</u>:

Diving:	450
Undercarriage down:	160
Flaps down:	140
Landing lamps lowered:	140

(ii) <u>A.S.R. dinghy</u>:

    Aircraft carrying air/sea rescue dinghy equipment must
    be fitted with an inertia weight in the elevator
    control circuit. Aerobatics and violent manoeuvres
    are not permitted until the equipment is dropped.

January 1942 A.P.1565B, Vol.I Sect.2
Amended by A.L.No.22/H

3. PRELIMINARIES

On entering the cockpit check:

Undercarriage selector lever – DOWN
(Check that indicator shows DOWN; switch on light indicator and check that green lights appear).

Flaps – UP

Landing lamps – UP

Contents of lower fuel tank.

4. STARTING THE ENGINE AND WARMING UP

(i) Set:

Both fuel cock levers – ON
Throttle – $\frac{1}{2}$ inch open
Mixture control – RICH
Airscrew speed control – Fully back DH 20°
Rotol 35° Propellor. Lever fully forward.
Radiator shutter – OPEN

(ii) Operate the priming pump to prime the suction and delivery pipes. This may be judged by a sudden increase in resistance of the plunger.

(iii) Prime the engine, the number of strokes required being as follows:

Air temperature °C:	+30	+20	+10	0	-10	-20
Normal fuel:	3	4	7	13		
High volatility fuel:				4	8	15

(iv) Switch ON ignition and pull out the priming pump handle.

(v) Press the starter push button and at the same time give one stroke of the priming pump. The push button also switches on the booster coil and should be kept depressed until the engine is firing evenly.

F.S/4

January 1942
Amended by A.L.No.22/H

> Note: If the engine fails to start on the first
> cartridge, no more priming should be carried out
> before firing the second, but another stroke
> should be given as the second cartridge is
> fired.

(vi) As soon as the engine is running evenly, screw down the priming pump.

5. TESTING ENGINE AND INSTALLATIONS

(i) While warming up, exercise the airscrew speed control a few times. Also make the usual checks of temperatures, pressures and controls. Brake pressure should be at least 120 lb/sq.in.

(ii) See that the cockpit hood is locked open and that the emergency exit door is set at the "half-clock" position.

(iii) After a few minutes move the airscrew speed control fully forward.

(iv) After warming up, open the throttle to give maximum boost for cruising with WEAK mixture and test the operation of the constant speed airscrew.

(v) Open the throttle to give maximum boost for cruising with RICH mixture and check each magneto in turn. The drop in r.p.m. should not exceed 150.

(vi) Open the throttle fully momentarily and check static r.p.m., boost and oil pressure.

(vii) Warming up must not be unduly prolonged because the radiator temperature before taxying out must not exceed 100°C.

When engines are being kept warm in readiness for immediate take-off, de Havilland 20° C.S. propeller should be left in fine pitch - control lever fully forward.

6. TAXYING OUT

It may be found that one wing tends to remain down while taxying. This is due to stiffness in the undercarriage leg, especially in a new aeroplane.

A.P.1565B, Vol.I Sect.2

FINAL PREPARATION FOR TAKE-OFF - DRILL OF VITAL ACTIONS

7. Drill is "T.M.P., Fuel, Flaps and Radiator".

> T - Trimming Tabs — Elevator about one division nose down from neutral. Rudder fully to starboard.
>
> M - Mixture control — RICH
>
> P - Pitch — Airscrew speed control fully forward.
>
> Fuel — Both cock levers ON and check contents of lower tank.
>
> Flaps — UP
>
> Radiator shutter — Fully open.

TAKE-OFF

8. (i) Open the throttle slowly to the gate (RATED BOOST position). Any tendency to swing can be counteracted by coarse use of the rudder. If taking off from a small aerodrome with a full load, max. boost may be obtained by opening the throttle through the gate to the TAKE-OFF BOOST position.

   (ii) After raising the undercarriage, see that the red indicator light - UP - comes on (it may be necessary to hold the lever hard forward against the quadrant until the indicator light comes on).

   (iii) Do not start to climb before a speed of 140 m.p.h. A.S.I.R. is attained.

CLIMBING

9. Up to 15,000 feet the maximum rate of climb is obtained at 160 m.p.h. A.S.I.R. but for normal climbing the following speeds are recommended:-

Ground level to 13,000 feet	185 m.p.h. A.S.I.R.
13,000 feet to 15,000 feet	180 " "
15,000 feet to 20,000 feet	160 " "
20,000 feet to 25,000 feet	140 " "
25,000 feet to 30,000 feet	125 " "
30,000 feet to 35,000 feet	110 " "

F.S/5

GENERAL FLYING

10. Stability and control

(i) This aeroplane is stable. With metal covered ailerons the lateral control is much lighter than with the earlier fabric covered ailerons and pilots accustomed to the latter must be careful not to overstress the wings. Similar care is necessary in the use of the elevators which are light and sensitive.

(ii) For normal cruising flight the radiator shutter should be in the minimum drag position.

(iii) Change of trim

    Undercarriage down - nose down
    Flaps down - nose down

(iv) Maximum range is obtained with WEAK mixture, 1,700 r.p.m. and at 160 m.p.h. A.S.I.R.

(v) Maximum endurance is obtained with WEAK mixture, 1,700 r.p.m. and at the lowest speed at which the machine can be comfortably flown.

(vi) For combat manoeuvres, climbing r.p.m. should be used.

(vii) For stretching a glide in the event of a forced landing, the airscrew speed control should be pulled right back and the radiator flap put at the minimum drag position.

STALLING

11. (i) At the stall one wing will usually drop with flaps either up or down and the machine may spin if the control column is held back.

(ii) This aeroplane has sensitive elevators and, if the control column is brought back too rapidly in a manoeuvre such as a loop or steep turn, stalling incidence may be reached and a high-speed stall induced. When this occurs there is a violent shudder and clattering noise throughout the aeroplane, which tends to flick over laterally and, unless the control column is put forward instantly, a rapid roll and spin will result.

(iii) Approximate stalling speeds when loaded to about 6,250 lb. are:-

    Flaps and undercarriage UP   73 m.p.h. A.S.I.R.
    " " " DOWN 64 " "

Issued with A.L.No.23/J   A.P.1565B, Vol.I Sect.2

SPINNING

12. (i) Spinning is permitted by pilots who have written permission from the C.O. of their squadron (C.F.I. of an O.T.U.). The loss of height involved in recovery may be very great, and the following height limits are to be observed:-

    (a) Spins are not to be started below 10,000 feet.

    (b) Recovery must be started not lower than 5,000 feet

    (ii) A speed of over 150 m.p.h. I.A.S. should be attained before starting to ease out of the resultant dive.

AEROBATICS

13. (i) This aeroplane is exceptionally good for aerobatics. Owing to its high performance and sensitive elevator control, care must be taken not to impose excessive loads either on the aeroplane or on the pilot and not to induce a high-speed stall. Many aerobatics may be done at much less than full throttle. Cruising r.p.m. should be used, because if reduced below this, detonation might occur if the throttle is opened up to climbing boost for any reason.

    (ii) The following speeds are recommended for aerobatics:-

    ### Looping

    Speed should be about 300 m.p.h. I.A.S. but may be reduced to 220-250 m.p.h. when the pilot is fully proficient.

    ### Rolling

    Speed should be anywhere between 180 and 300 m.p.h. I.A.S. The nose should be brought up about 30° above the horizon at the start, the roll being barrelled just enough to keep the engine running throughout.

    ### Half roll off loop

    Speed should be 320-350 m.p.h. I.A.S.

    ### Upward roll

    Speed should be about 350-400 m.p.h. I.A.S.

    ### Flick manoeuvres

    Flick manoeuvres are not permitted.

F.S/6

Amended by A.L.No.23/J	A.P.1565B, Vol.I Sect.2

(iv) If the green indicator light does not come on, hold the lever fully back for a few seconds. If this fails, raise the undercarriage and repeat the lowering. If this fails also, use the <u>emergency system</u> (see Section 1, Para. 12).

> Note: Before the emergency system can be used, the control lever must be in the down position. It may be necessary to push the nose down or invert the aeroplane in order to get the lever down.

(v) Correct speeds for the approach:-

Engine assisted	-	about 85 m.p.h. I.A.S.
Glide	-	" 90 " "

(vi) Sideslips may be performed quite satisfactorily with the flaps either up or down.

MISLANDING

15. Climb at about 120 m.p.h. I.A.S.

LANDING ACROSS WIND

16. The aeroplane can be landed across wind but it is undesirable that such landings should be made if the wind exceeds about 20 m.p.h.

AFTER LANDING

17. (i) After taxying in, set the propeller control fully back and open up the engine sufficiently to change pitch to coarse. DH 20°

  (ii) Allow the engine to idle for a few seconds, then pull the slow-running cut-out and hold it out until the engine stops.

  (iii) Turn OFF the fuel cocks and switch OFF the ignition.

FLYING AT REDUCED AIRSPEEDS

18. Reduce the speed to about 120 m.p.h. I.A.S. and lower the flaps. The radiator shutter must be opened to keep the temperature at about 100°C and the propeller speed control should be set to give cruising r.p.m.

F.S/7

Issued with A.L.No.23/J

POSITION ERROR TABLE

19. The corrections for position error are as follows:-

	m.p.h. I.A.S.										
From To	100 110	110 120	120 130	130 140	140 150	150 165	165 180	180 195	195 220	220 and over
Add Subtract	10	8	6	4	2	– –		2	4	6	8

FUEL AND OIL CAPACITY AND CONSUMPTION

20. (i) **Fuel and oil capacities**

> Fuel capacity:-
> 2 Main tanks - top tank   48 gallons
>   bottom tank   37 gallons
>
> Total effective capacity   85 gallons

> Oil capacity:-
> Effective capacity 5.8 gallons

(ii) **Fuel consumption**

Max r.p.m. and boost for:	Height feet	Approximate Consumption galls/hr.
Climbing	13,000	94
Cruising RICH	13,000	78
" WEAK	18,000	56
All-out level	14,500	98

OIL DILUTION IN COLD WEATHER

21. See A.P.2095/4. The dilution period should be:

Atmospheric temperatures above -10°C : $1\frac{1}{4}$ minutes
Atmospheric temperatures below -10°C : $2\frac{1}{2}$ minutes

Revised June, 1941
Issued with A.L.No.11

A.P.1565B, Vol.I and P.N., Introduction

INTRODUCTION

Note.- This Introduction and Sects.1 and 2 are also issued separately as "Pilot's Notes".

1. The Spitfire IIA or IIB is a single-seater fighter low-wing monoplane powered by a Merlin XII engine driving a Rotol or de Havilland variable-pitch airscrew which is governed by a constant-speed unit. The span of the aeroplane is 36 ft. 10 in. and the overall length is 29 ft. 11 in.

2. The Spitfire IIA and IIB differ only in armament, the Spitfire IIA having eight Browning .303 in. machine guns mounted in the main planes, and the Spitfire IIB having four Browning .303 in. machine guns and two Hispano 20 mm. cannon, also mounted in the main planes. The ammunition boxes for the machine guns each contain 300 rounds and are mounted in pairs between the guns. A drum-type magazine holding 60 rounds is fitted on each cannon.

3. The fuselage is of stressed-skin construction and consists of four main longerons, frames of either hoop or U-shape, and alclad plating stiffened between the frames by intercostals; the fin is an integral part of the tail end of the fuselage. The tail plane is also of stressed-skin construction, but the elevators, rudder and ailerons are of metal construction with fabric covering. The main planes are of single-spar stressed-skin construction with a light auxiliary spar and alclad and duralumin sheet covering; there is no centre section, the planes butting against the side of the fuselage. Split-trailing-edge flaps are fitted between the inboard ends of the ailerons and the fuselage sides.

4. The alighting gear consists of two separate retractable undercarriage units and a non-retractable tail wheel unit. The undercarriage units retract upwards and outwards into recesses in the undersurface of the main planes. Pneumatic wheel brakes and oleo-pneumatic shock-absorber struts are fitted.

5. The flying controls are of conventional type and the rudder pedals are adjustable horizontally for leg reach. The control column and rudder bar are connected to the control surfaces by cables. Trimming tabs, controllable from the cockpit, are fitted on the rudder and elevators.

6. The engine is mounted on a tubular structure attached to the fuselage front spar frame. Two fuel tanks, one above the other, are mounted in the fuselage forward of the cockpit. The oil tank is slung below the engine crankcase and two oil coolers, arranged one behind the other, are mounted on the underside of the port main plane. Pressure water-cooling is employed and the radiator is carried in a fairing on the underside of the starboard main plane; a flap, operated from the cockpit, is provided to control the flow of air through the radiator. The warm air from the radiator can be diverted through ducts

in the main planes, to the gun positions for heating the guns at high
altitudes. A Coffman cartridge starter is installed and there is no
hand-starting gear.

7. The hydraulic system for raising and lowering the undercarriage is operated by an engine-driven pump, but an emergency system
employing compressed carbon-dioxide is provided for lowering the
undercarriage. Compressed air for the pneumatic system is supplied by
an engine-driven compressor and two storage cylinders and operates the
trailing-edge flaps, the gun and camera gun firing and the lowering and
raising of the landing lamps, which are mounted on the undersurface of
the main planes.

8. Stowage for a parachute flare is provided in the fuselage.
A remotely-controlled combined transmitter-receiver is fitted behind
the pilot's seat. Power for the electrical services is derived from
an engine-driven generator and a 12-volt, 25-Ah. accumulator. A
carbon-pile regulator is fitted in the electrical system.

AIR PUBLICATION 1565B

SECTION 2

HANDLING AND FLYING NOTES FOR PILOT

	Para.
Engine Data	1
Flying Limitations	2
Preliminaries	3
Starting The Engine and Warming Up	4
Testing Engine and Installations	5
Taxying Out	6
Final Preparation For Take-off	7
Take-Off	8
Climbing	9
General Flying	10
Stalling	11
Spinning	12
Aerobatics	13
Diving	13a
Approach and Landing	14
Mislanding	15
Landing Across Wind	16
After Landing	17
Flying at Reduced Air Speeds	18
Position Error Table	19
Fuel and Oil Capacity and Consumption	20
Oil Dilution	21

FIGURES

Fuel System Diagram .. .. Fig 1

June, 1940

AIR PUBLICATION 1565B

Volume I

SECTION 2 – HANDLING AND FLYING NOTES FOR PILOT

LIST OF CONTENTS

	Para.
Introductory notes	1
Fitness of aeroplane for flight	2
Preliminaries	3
Starting the engine and warming up	4
Testing engine and installations	5
Taxying out	6
Final preparation for take-off – Drill of Vital Actions	7
Taking-off	8
Actions after taking-off	9
Engine failure during take-off	11
Climbing	12
The engine in cruising flight	13
General flying	14
Flying by instruments	15
Stalling	17
Spinning	18
Gliding	19
Sideslipping	20
Diving	21
Aerobatics	22
Combat manoeuvres	36
Approach and landing	41
Procedure after landing	49
Undercarriage EMERGENCY operation	50
Flying in rain and bad visibility	51
Forced landing owing to engine failure	53
Position error table	54
Notes concerning the Merlin XII engine	55
Fuel and oil capacity and consumptions	56

LIST OF ILLUSTRATIONS

	Fig.
Fuel system diagram	1

F.S./1

Amended in Vol.I by A.L.31
and in P.N. by A.L/L.

AIR PUBLICATION 1565B
Volume I and Pilot's Notes.

SECTION 2

HANDLING AND FLYING NOTES FOR PILOT

1. **ENGINE DATA: MERLIN XII**

   (i) **Fuel:** 100 octane (the reduced limitations for use with 87 octane fuel are shown in brackets)

   (ii) **Oil:** See A.P.1464/C.37.

   (iii) **Engine limitations:**

	R.p.m.	Boost lb/sq.in.	Temp. °C Clnt.	Oil.
MAX. TAKE-OFF TO 1,000 FEET	3,000	+12½(+7)	-	-
MAX. CLIMBING 1 HR. LIMIT	2,850	+ 9 (+7)	125	90
MAX. RICH CONTINUOUS	2,650	+ 7 (+5)	105*	90
MAX. WEAK CONTINUOUS	2,650	+ 4 (+2½)	105*	90
COMBAT 5 MINS. LIMIT	3,000	+12(+7)	135	105

   * 115°C. permitted for short periods if necessary.

   Note: +12 lb/sq.in. combat boost is obtained by operating the boost control cut-out and is effective up to about 10,500 feet.

   OIL PRESSURE: MINM. IN FLIGHT: 30 lb/sq.in.

   MINM. TEMP. FOR TAKE-OFF: OIL: 15°C
   COOLANT: 60°C

   FUEL PRESSURE: NORMAL: 2½-3 lb/sq.in.

F.S/3

(iv) <u>Other limitations</u>:
    Diving: Maximum r.p.m.: 3,600
    3,000 r.p.m. may be exceeded only for 20 seconds, with the throttle not less than one-third open.

(v) <u>Combat concession</u>:
3,000 r.p.m. may be used above 20,000 feet for periods not exceeding 30 minutes.

2. FLYING LIMITATIONS

(i) <u>Maximum speeds (m.p.h. I.A.S.)</u>:

    Diving: 450
    Undercarriage down: 160
    Flaps down: 140
    Landing lamps lowered: 140

(ii) <u>A.S.R. dinghy</u>:
Aircraft carrying air/sea rescue dinghy equipment must be fitted with an inertia weight in the elevator control circuit. Aerobatics and violent manoeuvres are not permitted until the equipment is dropped.

January 1942 A.P.1565B. Vol.I. Sect.2.
Amended by A.L.No.22/H.

3. PRELIMINARIES

On entering the cockpit check:

Undercarriage selector lever - DOWN
(Check that indicator shows DOWN; switch on light indicator and check that green lights appear).

Flaps - UP

Landing lamps - UP

Contents of lower fuel tank.

4. STARTING THE ENGINE AND WARMING UP

(i) Set:

Both fuel cock levers	- ON
Throttle	- ¼ inch open.
Mixture control	- RICH
Airscrew speed control	- Fully back
Radiator shutter	- OPEN

(ii) Operate the priming pump to prime the suction and delivery pipes. This may be judged by a sudden increase in resistance of the plunger.

(iii) Prime the engine, the number of strokes required being as follows:

Air temperature °C.:	+30	+20	+10	0	-10	-20
Normal fuel:		3	4	7	13	
High volatility fuel:				4	8	15

(iv) Switch ON ignition and pull out the priming pump handle.

(v) Press the starter push button and at the same time give one stroke of the priming pump. The push button also switches on the booster coil and should be kept depressed until the engine is firing evenly.

F.S/4

January 1942
Amended by A.L.No. 22/H.

> Note: If the engine fails to start on the first cartridge, no more priming should be carried out before firing the second, but another stroke should be given as the second cartridge is fired.

(vi) As soon as the engine is running evenly, screw down the priming pump.

5. TESTING ENGINE AND INSTALLATIONS.

(i) While warming up, exercise the airscrew speed control a few times. Also make the usual checks of temperatures, pressures and controls. Brake pressure should be at least 120 lb/sq.in.

(ii) See that the cockpit hood is locked open and that the emergency exit door is set at the "half-cock" position.

(iii) After a few minutes move the airscrew speed control fully forward.

(iv) After warming up, open the throttle to give maximum boost for cruising with WEAK mixture and test the operation of the constant speed airscrew.

(v) Open the throttle to give maximum boost for cruising with RICH mixture and check each magneto in turn. The drop in r.p.m. should not exceed ~~100~~ 150

(vi) Open the throttle fully momentarily and check static r.p.m., boost and oil pressure.

(vii) Warming up must not be unduly prolonged because the radiator temperature before taxying out must not exceed 100°C.

6. TAXYING OUT

It may be found that one wing tends to remain down while taxying. This is due to stiffness in the undercarriage leg, especially in a new aeroplane.

A.P.1565B, Vol.I, Sect.2

taking off, due to the throttle coming back when his hand is not on the throttle lever (when raising the undercarriage).

(d) <u>Clearing engine before take-off</u>.- The engine should not be allowed to idle too slowly, and should be "cleared" before taking off by opening up to moderate r.p.m. against the brakes, care being taken to hold the stick fully back, and not to raise the tail by opening up to too high a power. Ensure that the maximum temperature limit is not exceeded ($120^{\circ}C$.).

FINAL PREPARATION FOR TAKE-OFF - DRILL OF VITAL ACTIONS

7. On reaching the take-off position, stop across wind, facing the aerodrome circuit, and carry out the Drill of Vital Actions. Some of this may already have been done, but must invariably be checked before every take-off. A convenient catch-phrase is applied to this drill "T.M.P. and Flaps".

(i)	- T -	Trimming tabs	- Elevator about one division nose down from neutral. Rudder about central or, if preferred fully to starboard.
(ii)	- M -	Mixture control	- Back to NORMAL
(iii)	- P - and	Pitch control	- FULLY FINE (lever fully forward)
		Flaps	- UP (These must never be down when taking-off, as they would be at 85°).

<u>Note</u>.- The aeroplane would, however, take-off with flaps down, and if, by a serious omission of drill, the pilot leaves them down, he must on no account raise them until speed is at least 120 m.p.h. A.S.I. at a safe height.

TAKING-OFF

8. Turn into wind, steady the aeroplane, and move forward slowly to straighten up the tail wheel; then open to full throttle and take-off by holding the aeroplane to a constant attitude. The tail need not be raised much - the take-off run is only about 150 yards, and the time less than 9 seconds. Any tendency to swing left can easily be counteracted by coarse rudder control. Hold down almost to level flight.

F.S./6

Amended by A.L.No.3

ACTIONS AFTER TAKING-OFF

9. Proceed as follows:-

Immediate actions.- After taking-off carry out the following Drill of Vital Actions. Catch-phrase - "U.P."

(i) As soon as the aeroplane is <u>FINALLY</u> clear of the ground, wait for a few seconds (not more than about five) to ensure that the aeroplane is gathering speed, and that it will not touch the ground again, and then, after observing carefully that the aeroplane is several feet clear, especially if the aerodrome surface rises,

U - <u>Raise the undercarriage</u>. On no account must the climb be started at this stage; the aeroplane should be held **almost** to level flight until a safe speed of 140 m.p.h. A.S.I. is reached (it should then be, roughly speaking between 10 to 20 feet clear of the ground or obstructions). Ensure that the red indicator light - UP - comes on (it may be necessary to hold the lever hard forward against the quadrant until the indicator comes ON)

(ii) Then start a gradual climb, throttle down to the rated (+9 lb./sq.in. boost) position and:-

P - Move pitch control back to give 2,850 r.p.m.

(iii) Continue to accelerate until the airspeed reaches a climbing speed of 185 m.p.h. A.S.I. at +9 lb./sq.in. boost and then adjust the attitude to maintain this speed.

Subsequent actions.- These may be performed at leisure, though without undue delay.

(iv) Observe oil pressure (60 lb./sq.in.). The habit should be formed of looking at this first and foremost. An engine can seize up in less than a minute if the oil pressure fails.

(v) Fully close the emergency exit door and then close the cockpit hood.

(vi) Close the radiator shutter (unless a high power climb is done, when the lever should be a little forward).

(vii) Make any further adjustments to the engine and airscrew controls as desired.

(viii) Note the radiator and oil temperatures.

(ix) Look round the cockpit systematically.

10. Feet may be taken off the rudder control to save fatigue, as its use is only necessary when taking-off, landing, flying at low speed or aerobatics. Even aerobatics, such as rolls, can be done with feet clear of the rudder control, but rudder would be needed

Issued with A.L.No.23/J.   A.P.1565B. Vol.I,Sect.2.

SPINNING.

12.(i) Spinning is permitted by pilots who have written permission from the C.O. of their squadron (C.F.I. of an O.T.U.). The loss of height involved in recovery may be very great, and the following height limits are to be observed:-

    (a) Spins are not to be started below 10,000 feet.

    (b) Recovery must be started not lower than 5,000 feet.

(ii) A speed of over 150 m.p.h. I.A.S. should be attained before starting to ease out of the resultant dive.

AEROBATICS.

13.(i) This aeroplane is exceptionally good for aerobatics. Owing to its high performance and sensitive elevator control, care must be taken not to impose excessive loads either on the aeroplane or on the pilot and not to induce a high-speed stall. Many aerobatics may be done at much less than full throttle. Cruising r.p.m. should be used, because if reduced below this, detonation might occur if the throttle is opened up to climbing boost for any reason.

(ii) The following speeds are recommended for aerobatics:-

Looping.- Speed should be about 300 m.p.h. I.A.S. but may be reduced to 220-250 m.p.h. when the pilot is fully proficient.

Rolling.- Speed should be anywhere between 180 and 300 m.p.h. I.A.S. The nose should be brought up about 30° above the horizon at the start, the roll being barrelled just enough to keep the engine running throughout.

Half roll off loop.- Speed should be 320-350 m.p.h. I.A.S.

Upward roll.- Speed should be about 350-400 m.p.h. I.A.S.

Flick manoeuvres.- Flick manoeuvres are not permitted.

F.S/6.

Amended by A.L.No.23/J.

DIVING

13a.(i) The aeroplane becomes very tail heavy at high speed and must be trimmed into the dive in order to avoid the dangers of excessive acceleration in recovery. The forward trim should be wound back as speed is lost after pulling out.

(ii) A tendency to yaw to the right should be corrected by use of the rudder trimming tab.

APPROACH AND LANDING.

14.(i) During the preliminary approach see that the cockpit hood is locked open, and the emergency exit door is set at half-cock position. Take care not to get the arm out into the airflow.

(ii) Reduce speed to 140 m.p.h. I.A.S. and carry out the Drill of Vital Actions "U.M.P. and flaps".

    U - Undercarriage - DOWN (Watch indicators and check green lights)

    M - Mixture control - RICH

    P - Pitch - Propeller speed control fully forward.

    Flaps - DOWN

(iii) When lowering the undercarriage hold the lever fully forward for about two seconds. This will take the weight off the locking pins and allow them to turn freely when the lever is pulled back. The lever should then be pulled back smartly to the down position; if it cannot be pulled fully back, hold it forward again for at least two seconds. If it becomes jammed it may generally be released by a smart blow of the hand. If this fails it is necessary to take the weight of the wheels off the locking pins, either by pushing the nose down sharply or by inverting the aeroplane. The lever can then be pulled straight back.

Amended by A.L.No.23/J.　　　A.P.1565B. Vol.I, Sect.2.

(iv) If the green indicator light does not come on, hold the lever fully back for a few seconds. If this fails, raise the undercarriage and repeat the lowering. If this fails also, use the <u>emergency system</u> (see Section 1, Para.12).

Note: Before the emergency system can be used, the control lever must be in the down position. It may be necessary to push the nose down or invert the aeroplane in order to get the lever down.

(v) Correct speeds for the approach:-

    Engine assisted - about 85 m.p.h. I.A.S.
    Glide   -   " 90 "   "

(vi) Sideslips may be performed quite satisfactorily with the flaps either up or down.

MISLANDING.

15. Climb at about 120 m.p.h. I.A.S.

LANDING ACROSS WIND.

16. The aeroplane can be landed across wind but it is undesirable that such landings should be made if the wind exceeds about 20 m.p.h.

AFTER LANDING.

17.(i) After taxying in, set the propeller control fully back and open up the engine sufficiently to change pitch to coarse. (D.H. 20° ~~~)

(ii) Allow the engine to idle for a few seconds, then pull the slow-running cut-out and hold it out until the engine stops.

(iii) Turn OFF the fuel cocks and switch OFF the ignition.

FLYING AT REDUCED AIRSPEEDS.

18. Reduce the speed to about 120 m.p.h. I.A.S. and lower the flaps. The radiator shutter must be opened to keep the temperature at about $100°C$ and the propeller speed control should be set to give cruising r.p.m.

F.S/7.

Issued with A.L.No.23/J.

POSITION ERROR TABLE.

19. The corrections for position error are as follows:-

	m.p.h. I.A.S.								
From	100	110	120	130	140	150	165	180	195	220 and
To	110	120	130	140	150	165	180	195	220	over
Add Subtract	10	8	6	4	2	– –	2	4	6	8

FUEL AND OIL CAPACITY AND CONSUMPTION.

20.(i) <u>Fuel and oil capacities.</u>-

Fuel capacity:-
2 Main tanks - top tank   48 gallons
bottom tank   37 gallons
Total effective capacity   85 gallons

Oil capacity:-
Effective capacity 5.8 gallons.

(ii) <u>Fuel consumption</u>:-

Max r.p.m. and boost for:	Height feet.	Approximate Consumption galls/hr.
Climbing	13,000	94
Cruising RICH	13,000	78
" WEAK	18,000	56
All-out level	14,500	98

OIL DILUTION IN COLD WEATHER

21. See A.P.2095/4. The dilution period should be:

Atmospheric temperatures above $-10^{\circ}C$: $1\frac{1}{4}$ minutes
Atmospheric temperatures below $-10^{\circ}C$: $2\frac{1}{2}$ minutes.

A.P.1565B, Vol.I, Sect.2

(vii) **Flaps**.- The flaps must be UP at speeds over 120 m.p.h. A.S.I. If this speed is exceeded with flaps DOWN, they will partially retract.

SIDESLIPPING

20. This aeroplane sideslips quite satisfactorily with the flaps UP or DOWN. Maintain speed (slightly above the normal gliding speed) when sideslipping.

DIVING

21. The maximum permissible diving speed is 450 m.p.h. A.S.I. Note the following:-

(i) **Constant-speed airscrew**.- At maximum r.p.m. 3,000, the throttle must be 1/3 open. The pitch control need not be brought back to reduce r.p.m., the range of pitch is enough to hold down the r.p.m. at any airspeed.

(ii) The flaps must be up at over 120 m.p.h. A.S.I.

(iii) The aeroplane should be trimmed in the dive, i.e. the trimming tab control should be set to give no load on the elevator. This will lessen the possibility of excessive "g" being induced in easing out of the dive particularly if the pilot should release his hold on the stick owing to "blacking-out" or any other reasons. No difficulty in easing out of the dive will be experienced even if the aeroplane is trimmed in the dive as the elevator control is comparatively light and recovery from the dive is not resisted by excessive stability in pitch. Elevator tabs may be used, very carefully, as described in para.14.

(iv) The rate of descent is very great, so ample height must be allowed for recovery.

AEROBATICS

22. **General remarks**.- The Spitfire is an exceptionally good aeroplane for aerobatics, but spinning is prohibited and aerobatics must not be performed below 5,000 ft. Aerobatics on this aeroplane may be done only by pilots who have adequate flying experience of the aeroplane and who have written authority from their Squadron Commander. The Air Ministry and local regulations in force must be rigidly obeyed.

F.S./10

23. **Characteristics and precautions.-** The chief characteristics of this aeroplane affecting aerobatics, and the precautions necessary are as follows:-

(i) High speed in the dive. This, coupled with the fact that the very effective elevator control, and comparative instability in pitch of this aeroplane, makes it very easy for the pilot to impose high load-factors, or "g", when looping, doing tight turns, or pulling out of a dive. Although the safety factor of the aeroplane is about 10, it is well within the pilot's power to exceed "10g"; the wings would certainly fail if this figure is much exceeded. In very bumpy atmosphere, care is needed when manoeuvring with high "g", to prevent the arm from jerking the stick, owing to the jerking of the body in bumps, causing sudden fluctuations of "g", between about "2g" and "6g". A sudden upward bump bends the pilot's body and jerks the stick back, unless he jams his elbow against his body or the side of the cockpit.

(ii) Rapid loss of height in a dive. An ample margin of height must be allowed for diving either deliberately or if there is any chance of an accidental dive.

(iii) Great loss of height in the event of loss of control, such as a complete stall, flick roll, or spin. This is not only because of the rapid loss of height when stalled, or spinning, but also because of the need for gathering ample speed in the recovery dive, before beginning to ease out, owing to the fact that a semi-stalled condition of the wings persists well above stalling speed, and premature pulling out will cause another "flick", or a spin.

(iv) The high wing loading of the aeroplane. This is the chief cause of the characteristics already mentioned.

(v) Rather too effective elevator control and instability in pitch at large angles of attack (when turning or looping at high "g"). The results are already described in sub-para.(i).

(vi) Violent stall at high speed. Severe shudder and clatter is produced if the aeroplane is stalled at high speed (see para.17).

(vii) Great reserve of power.

(viii) Effective aileron control at all speeds down to the stall. It is, at the same time, excessively heavy at high speed. It should not be used with too much strength at very high speed, as it tends to twist the wings, which may already be under high torsional stress.

Note the following:-

(i) The elevator trimming tab may be used, either in the loop or in the recovery from the dive, but, if so, great care must be taken to move it slowly and not to continue moving it back beyond the point giving about "3g". Remember too, that if a vertical dive is started at a slow speed with the tab control too far back, (for example, if the speed gets too slow on the top of the loop, and the aeroplane is allowed to fall into a dive without "flicking-out"), the "g", or load factor, will rapidly become excessive as the aeroplane gathers speed.

(ii) The Rocket Loop, Large Loop, and other variations may also be done effectively.

(iii) The following example of the airspeed at various stages of a typical loop may be of interest:-

		Start	—	300 m.p.h. A.S.I.
$90°$	—	Vertical	—	200 m.p.h. A.S.I.
$180°$	—	Inverted	—	115 m.p.h. A.S.I.
$360°$	—	Level	—	290 m.p.h. A.S.I.

26. **Rolling.-** Rolling is very easy, though the aileron control is extremely heavy at high speed. It may even be done with feet off the rudder pedals, if it is "barrelled" a little, - that is, a <u>slight</u> amount of positive pitch (or loop) maintained during the roll. Rolling is done in the normal way, as described in the Flying Training Manual, Chapter III. A roll may be either moderately slow, slow, or barrel, ("slow" refers to rate of roll, not airspeed). The moderately slow roll is the best, as the engine can be kept running normally throughout. It should be started at a speed of anything over about 160 m.p.h. A.S.I. Slower speed than this is possible, even down to 110 m.p.h., but at this extreme there is danger of stalling and spinning if the stick is pulled back at all. At higher speeds than 200 m.p.h. or so, aileron control becomes excessively heavy, and at 300 m.p.h. or over the roll should be done extremely slowly, by easing the nose up $30°$ or $40°$ above the horizon and then using only enough aileron control to roll slowly, avoiding the use of any considerable force. The best method, to keep the engine running, is to ease the nose up to about $20°$ or $30°$ above the horizon, and then start the roll at moderate rate by aileron control, assisted, if desired, by a little rudder at first; (this is unnecessary). As the aeroplane rolls on to its back it must be kept straight, and the nose allowed to come down very slightly, but <u>not below the horizon</u>. As the aeroplane rolls out, top rudder should be used to keep the nose up, aileron control used, as required, to steady the roll (that is, to check any tendency to roll out quickly) and the aeroplane kept straight so that the nose is pointing just above the horizon in the original direction after the roll. First attempts should be made with slight barrelling - the roll started with the nose about $30°$ up, and the nose allowed to come down <u>almost</u> on to the horizon

A.P.1565B, Vol.I, Sect. 2

24. General precautions.- Note the following:-

(i) The pilot should ensure that the harness is tight enough, and be especially careful, for inverted flying, that it is not caught up in any way. This frequently happens, and causes the pilot's body to drop suddenly an inch or two, when the kink frees itself. This is most disconcerting.

(ii) See that the neighbouring sky, especially below, is clear of aircraft.

(iii) Do not use more power or higher r.p.m. than is necessary - on no account exceed the limits laid down. Many aerobatics, such as rolls, may be done at much less than full throttle. Cruising r.p.m. should be used (2,850) - if reduced below this, detonation might occur if the throttle is opened up to +9 lb./sq.in. boost, for any reason.

(iv) Use too high a speed rather than too low, especially when doing aerobatics on this aircraft for the first time, as there is then less likelihood of losing control; but handle the aeroplane correspondingly more carefully at the higher speeds.

(v) Do not continue any manoeuvre if vision fades owing to high "g", (see further remarks under Looping, para.25).

25. Looping.- This should be started at not less than about 300 m.p.h. A.S.I. When thoroughly proficient the pilot can do it at slower speed, but there will then be a tendency to get too slow on the top, with a consequent likelihood of a flick-out or spin when the angle of attack is brought to stalling incidence if the stick is pulled back too far. Large loops may be started at any speed up to the maximum permissible, but the beginning of the loop must then be EXTREMELY GRADUAL, and the elbow pressed into the body or leg to prevent jerking of the over-sensitive elevator control in bumps. The method of looping is normal, (see Flying Training Manual, Chapter III). The pilot should endeavour to maintain constant "g", that is, to tighten up the start of the loop very gradually to about "3g", and then maintain this by very gradually continuing to tighten up the loop as speed decreases. The pilot has no way of telling the value of "g", but a rough guide is that the average pilot begins to lose vision at about "$4\frac{1}{2}$g", and so, if the loop is done well short of this "blacking out" point, it will be about "3g" or so. When loss of vision is approaching the pilot will experience a sensation of downward pull behind the eyes and ears, and vision will begin to fade. No manoeuvre should be continued if sight is lost, as the pilot loses one of his guides to the rate of loop, and might increase "g" to the point where the brain fails altogether or the wings break.

F.S./11

A.P.1565B, Vol.I, Sect.2

when inverted, and, as the aeroplane rolls out, to come <u>slightly</u> round the horizon and then up a little as the aeroplane levels. When proficient, the pilot will be able to cut out this barrelling completely, keeping the nose straight, just above the horizon, throughout the roll, the engine continuing to run. If the engine shows signs of beginning to fade, the stick should be brought back a little, almost imperceptibly.

27. <u>The true slow roll</u>.- This can be done, if high speed is used at the start, but the engine will cut when inverted. This is done in the normal way, the nose being kept pointing straight in a constant direction, except when the wings are vertical at the start and finish, when it should be raised a little by top rudder, to prevent loss of height. If the engine is throttled back as the roll is started, it will be possible to get the engine going again earlier in the final stages of the roll.

28. <u>The barrel roll</u>.- This may be done with feet off the rudder, and is an exaggeration of the barrel type of moderate slow roll already described.

29. <u>A series of rolls</u>.- These can be done very easily on this aeroplane, either to left or right, at about 0 lb./sq.in. boost, and cruising r.p.m. at a speed of about 180 m.p.h. A.S.I. (or even less - 160 m.p.h.). They should be barrelled at first, the rate of roll being slowed down in the last quarter of each roll to regain speed lost when the nose was up; but when proficient, the pilot can do these with the nose up about $10°$ or so with very little barrelling.

30. <u>Climbing rolls and gliding rolls</u>.- These can also be done, the principles being the same. In doing gliding rolls, on a slightly down hill path, the pilot must be careful not to let the nose drop into a steep dive, and then pull out roughly. They are the most difficult type of roll to do properly.

31. <u>Upward roll</u>.- This is a useful exercise, but should not be overdone - on no account should the engine be over-revved; but speed at the start should be high, and the aeroplane eased up very gradually at first. When pointing vertically, rudder may be used to assist aileron, but not enough to deflect the nose appreciably. Do not hold the vertical attitude too long (watch the airspeed and start "recovery" while speed is still well over 100 m.p.h. A.S.I.). Otherwise a tail slide will result, which may break the control surfaces or connections, unless these are held rigidly central, which may be impossible. Finish off by cartwheeling and quarter rolling, or by allowing the nose to drop forward (not sharply enough to stop the engine), or by completing a loop to the inverted position and half-rolling out.

F.S./12

32. **Downward roll.-** This is useful in combat, at the start of a vertical dive, before speed has become excessive. Rolls may be done equally well either to left or right, and pilots should practise this to avoid becoming "one-sided".

33. **Half roll off the top of the loop.-** The loop should be started with more speed than for a plain loop, and the roll begun directly the opposite horizon comes into view, as the pilot looks "up" through the dome of the hood, while the nose is still about $30°$ or $40°$ above the horizon. It should be regulated in such a way that the nose continues to come down gradually, as the aeroplane rolls out, until it is just above the horizon at the end. This will keep the engine running and ensure that the aircraft continues to gain height during the roll out. The aeroplane should then be travelling on exactly the opposite course to its original. This also may be done equally well to left or right. The pilot's weight should not come on to the shoulder straps at any time.

34. **Flick manoeuvres.-** The high-speed variety of flick-roll or flick half-roll must ON NO ACCOUNT be done. It is liable to cause severe strain, is clumsy and uncomfortable, and, being extremely easy, has no training or other value of any kind. But a flick-roll at low speed, and low r.p.m. done very gently, is a useful exercise in timing and control at low speeds, and prevention of spin. It is done by throttling well back, slowing down to about 140 m.p.h. A.S.I., and then very gently easing the stick back and, at the same time, applying rudder. The nose will rise and yaw, and, as the control angles are steadily increased, the aeroplane will suddenly start to "auto-rotate", or flick. If the stick is kept back the aircraft would then spin, but, as soon as the aeroplane approaches an even keel (at about the moment when the wings are vertical) the stick is put forward, and, as the flick ceases, the controls used to steady the aeroplane until the roll is completed. If this is done too late the aeroplane will continue to flick, until it does part of a turn of a spin; if done too soon the flick will stop, and the rest of the roll must be done by aileron control, in the normal way.

ON NO ACCOUNT CARRY OUT FLICK MANOEUVRES EXCEPT AT LOW SPEEDS, but remember that low speed makes spinning more likely if the controls are mishandled. Ample height should be allowed (see Stalling and Spinning, paras. 17 and 18). Other variations of loops, rolls and so on may be carried out.

35. **Inverted flying.-** This is normal. Ensure that the harness is tight, and follow each strap to its attachment to ensure that it has a straight "run" and is not doubled over or caught up. Keep the seat well down to avoid bumping the head. Do not use rudder control when turning inverted. It is best to half-roll into and out of the inverted position. If recovery is made in a half-loop, the elevator tab should be used, very carefully, as the aeroplane may tend to get nose heavy as it gathers speed. DO NOT trim with the tab when inverted, for this reason - keep the nose up by the necessary force on the elevator control, if the aeroplane is nose-heavy. Do not fly inverted unless provision is made to

A.P.1565B, Vol.I, Sect.2

prevent fouling the engine and aircraft with oil or coolant. Watch oil pressure, and do not open up the engine again until oil pressure is restored.

COMBAT MANOEUVRES

36. Aerobatics, though vitally important as training for mastery of the aeroplane, and for tactical manoeuvres, are not of the slightest use for such manoeuvre and combat, if carried out as <u>aerobatics.</u> That is to say, they are none of them used, because they are too slow, except one or two of the simplest when merged into simple, smooth and rapid changes of position.

37. In air fighting the pilot, when climbing or manoeuvring for position <u>before</u> the attack, must obtain the last ounce of performance from his aeroplane. Aerobatics are not the quickest way of getting from position A to position B in the air. When actually attacking, the pilot concentrates on nothing else except bringing his guns to bear on the target. Therefore all his manoeuvres are simple turns, or a smooth combination of pitch and roll merged uniformly into one another. To give two examples:-

(i) If the pilot wishes to attack an enemy aircraft passing 500 ft. overhead on an opposite course, he does <u>NOT</u> do a half-loop followed by a half-roll - it takes too long; he makes a quick, smooth, and absolutely uniform climbing turn in the best direction (not necessarily free from skidding, if this will help speed up the turn without loss of speed).

(ii) Diving on to an enemy is done in the simplest and quickest way - by a swift and smooth roll, turn, cartwheel, dive and pull-out all merged into one - <u>NOT</u> by a complete half-roll followed by a quarter loop, and perhaps half a downward roll and pull-out,"by numbers" - it would take longer. <u>The simplest possible manoeuvre is the most efficient.</u>

38. <u>Turning circle.</u>- Never attempt a "tail-chase" with an enemy aeroplane having a smaller turning circle that the Spitfire. It is likely that most aircraft of lesser top speed (though it does not necessarily depend on that, but rather on stalling speed and other things) will be able to out-turn the Spitfire. Therefore the pilot should break off an attack the instant his gun-sights cease to "bear". It is not intended here to say more about fighter tactics, but this is a matter concerning the aerodynamic control of the aeroplane. If a turn of the smallest diameter, or at the quickest rate of change of direction <u>is</u> required at any time, the pilot must not tighten it up too closely to the stalling incidence. Even if the aeroplane does not begin to shudder or otherwise indicate an imminent stall, it may not be turning quite as quickly as it would if the stick is very slightly eased forward. If stalling incidence is

F.S./13

reached, the aeroplane usually does a violent shudder, with a loud "clattering" noise, and comes out of the turn with a violent flick. This would be a serious loss of advantage in a combat.

39. **Manoeuvreability.-** Manoeuvreability in combat consists of two separate and distinct features:-

(i) Quickness of rate of change of direction, or rate of turn - and, secondary to this, smallness of turning circle (treated above). Very roughly speaking, this is a function of the stalling speed, - that is, an aeroplane with a high stalling speed has a large turning circle.

(ii) Quickness of change of attitude - that is, shortness of time necessary to go from straight flight to vertical bank. Seconds may be gained at the beginning of a tail-chase by light and effective aileron control. An aeroplane cannot reach its best rate of turn until it is in a vertical bank (though bank must, of course, be reduced to less than the vertical if the turn is sustained for more than about $180°$). The Spitfire is not good in this respect; its aileron control is very heavy at high speed (over 300 m.p.h.) and rudder should be used to assist rapid roll, if necessary.

40. **Blacking-out.-** Never increase the load factor, or "g", in tightening up a turn or loop, or pulling out of a dive, to such an extent that loss of vision (or "blacking-out") occurs. It has several disadvantages:-

(i) It is dangerous, partly because it may lead to complete unconsciousness if "g" is further increased, and partly because the pilot loses all guides to the control of the aeroplane except his (often misleading) physical senses, and may either (supposing he is in a steep dive) fail to complete pulling out, and continue into the ground, or pull out too quickly, - quite easy to do owing to the rather over-effective elevator of the Spitfire, coupled with this aeroplane's comparative lack of stability in pitch, - this might result in complete unconsciousness or break-up of the aeroplane.

(ii) The pilot is immediately at a disadvantage. In combat he loses sight of the enemy, and at any time he cannot complete the manoeuvre efficiently.

Note.- Every pilot should practise subjecting himself to high "g", but **short** of the blacking-out point. This will increase his capacity to withstand it, and give him an advantage over an opponent who blacks-out at a lower "g" than he does.

APPROACH AND LANDING

41. **General remarks.-** The landing must always be made with flaps DOWN. This aeroplane, in spite of its high speed, is very easy to land. The following features are mentioned:-

(i) Rather bad view straight ahead; the pilot's head is lower than in the Hurricane relative to the engine.

(ii) Steep angle of descent. When gliding speed is low the aeroplane may appear to have insufficient speed to flatten out, but when it comes near the ground, cushioning effect causes considerable "float" unless speed is the minimum.

42. **Preliminary approach.-** General preparations for landing should be made, while the aeroplane nears the aerodrome; these include:-

(i) Open and lock back the cockpit hood.

(ii) Ensure that the mixture control is back to NORMAL.

(iii) Stow maps.

Note.- There is no need to open the radiator shutter, provided flying at low speed is not unduly prolonged. The correct drill avoids this.

43. **Drill of Vital Actions before landing.-** This should be carried out quickly and decisively when the right moment arrives, when approaching the lee side of the aerodrome. A convenient catch-phrase is applied to this drill, "U.P. and Flaps", that is:-

(i) - U - Undercarriage - DOWN (Watch indicators and ensure that the green light comes ON, see note below)

(ii) - P - Pitch and - fully FINE (Lever fully forward)

(iii) - Flaps - DOWN (This should not be done before the aeroplane turns in towards the aerodrome to land).

Note.- If the undercarriage green indicator light does not come ON the control lever should be held back and down hard against the quadrant and still in the LOWER position. When the light comes ON the lever may be released to allow the cut-out to return the unit to IDLE. Of all the indicators are not showing the undercarriage to be fully down and locked, or if there is still doubt, the control lever should be returned firmly to the RAISE position. When the red UP indicator light comes ON, the LOWER movement should be repeated. If the indicators still do not show the undercarriage to be fully down and locked, the emergency lowering system should be used.

44. **Methods of approach and landing.-** This aeroplane can easily be landed without the assistance of the engine, and, when there is ample room and conditions are good, this method is recommended, in order that the pilot can be fully at home in case of a forced landing. (Gliding speed about 90 m.p.h. A.S.I.). Otherwise, the normal method is the Engine-assisted approach, in which the engine is used to regulate the approach (which should

NOT be on a flat path, but almost on a glide path) and then, at a fast tick-over, to flatten the glide path and reduce the rate of descent; throttle back immediately <u>after</u> flattening out. (Gliding speed with engine, 80 to 85 m.p.h. A.S.I.). These two methods can be combined, for practice, the engine-assisted approach being used down to 500 ft. (no lower) and the aeroplane brought within gliding distance, engine shut off, and glide and landing made without engine (glide about 90 m.p.h. A.S.I.). Lastly there is the Creeper, a method, <u>only to be used in emergency</u>, for landing in a small field, by flying in close to the ground at minimum safe speed, closing the throttles as the lee boundary is crossed (but only after getting close to the ground) and landing.

45. <u>Three-point landing</u>.- The stick should be brought right back in landing (but this must not be misjudged and brought right back if the pilot is uncertain how high up - one foot or five feet - the aeroplane is). The tail comes down satisfactorily, in fact, if the stick is brought right back before the aeroplane touches, with the wheels a few inches off the ground, the tail wheel will sometimes run 100 yds. on the ground before the main wheels touch. This may be due to the cushioning effect of the air between the wings and the ground.

46. <u>Wheel brakes.</u>- These should always be used with care, but can generally be put almost full on without lifting the tail. It is a good plan to get into the habit of gripping the ring-grip on the stick with the third and little fingers and thumb and the break lever with the first and second fingers only. This facilitates quick release in case the tail lifts, without a tendency to let the stick go forward.

47. <u>Mislanding</u>.- Open up to full throttle and remain in the air. <u>Do not raise the flaps</u> until a speed of 120 m.p.h. is attained (at a safe height, though there will be no sink at this speed).

48. <u>Landing across wind</u>.- This aeroplane can be landed across wind, but, unless the pilot is very skilful in eliminating drift, it should not be attempted in too high a wind owing to the narrow-track undercarriage. Drift may be eliminated either by:-

(i) Sideslipping.

(ii) Flat turn towards the drift at the moment of landing.

<u>Note</u>.- For full details of the latest technique of approach and landing, applicable to modern aeroplanes, <u>see</u> Flying Training Manual. Part I, Chapter III.

PROCEDURE AFTER LANDING

49. Immediately after landing, look round to ensure that no aircraft are coming in, and taxy clear of the landing area, to the aerodrome perimeter. Then stop, and proceed as follows:-

A.P.1565B, Vol.I, Sect.2

(i) Raise flaps.

(ii) Open radiator shutter.

(iii) Taxy in. Run the engine slowly for about a minute, before or after turning OFF fuel cocks. Pull out the slow-running cut-out and hold until engine stops, then switch OFF.

(iv) Switch OFF indicator lights and all other electrical switches.

UNDERCARRIAGE EMERGENCY OPERATION

50. A CO_2 cylinder is provided to supply pressure to force the undercarriage down in case of failure of the normal system. The system is independent of the latter, except the mechanical parts of the undercarriage units.

(i) *Method of use*.- The undercarriage is lowered and finally locked down by first selecting CHASSIS DOWN with the normal selector lever and then pushing the emergency lever, painted RED, forwards and downwards (through a little more than a right angle); this causes a pin to puncture the CO_2 cylinder. After use of the emergency system the following action is necessary:-

(a) Replace the CO_2 cylinder and seal the lever.

(b) Inspect, rectify and refill the normal hydraulic system. (If the emergency system has been used accidentally, and there has been no failure of the normal system, refilling only will be necessary.)

FLYING IN RAIN AND BAD VISIBILITY

51. When flying in conditions of bad visibility with the ground in sight, or if flying in formation, open the cockpit hood if the view becomes too bad with it closed. A break-out panel is fitted to the cockpit hood which can be pushed out by a blow with the elbow, with the heel of the hand or fist, if for any reason, such as severe ice-accretion, the hood cannot be opened. It is advisable, in order to facilitate navigation and to obviate the risk of collision with suddenly rising ground, greatly to reduce speed. In extreme cases flaps may be lowered and the aeroplane flown at as low a speed as 120 m.p.h. A.S.I. Radiator shutter must be opened (radiator temperature will stabilize at about 100°C) and the airscrew should be set to give about 1,500 r.p.m. If

F.S./15

conditions are such that higher speed is safe, then the flaps should be raised, and the throttle set to give a speed of about 180 m.p.h. A.S.I. Lowering the undercarriage, <u>with flaps up</u> enables a slightly lower speed to be maintained, 160 m.p.h A.S.I. The flaps cannot be lowered to increase drag above 120 m.p.h. A.S.I. because they affect the flow of air to the radiator, and cause the engine temperature to rise above the limit.

<u>Note</u>.- <u>Flaps up</u>. Reduce speed to about 180 m.p.h. and set the airscrew pitch as coarse as will allow smooth running.

<u>Flaps down</u>. 120 m.p.h. - pitch set to give higher r.p.m. than above. Watch temperatures.

52. Flying with the undercarriage down might be necessary for purposes of recognition as a friendly aircraft; this is satisfactory, as the undercarriage has far less drag than the flaps.

FORCED LANDING OWING TO ENGINE FAILURE

<u>Note</u>.- <u>See</u> also para.11 - "Engine failure during take-off".

53. The principles of forced landing this aeroplane are the same as for any other type, the first actions being to maintain ample gliding speed, select a landing ground, glide towards it and then try to rectify the trouble. If a landing without engines is inevitable, act as follows:-

(i) Switch off the engine and put fuel cocks down to OFF.

(ii) Decide whether the undercarriage is to be used or not and act accordingly.

<u>Note</u>.- The question of whether or not to lower the undercarriage is decided by the size and surface of the landing ground, bearing in mind that a landing on the fuselage does far less damage than turning over.

IF IN DOUBT, LAND WITH UNDERCARRIAGE UP.

It is a partial air brake, and so should be left up to extend the initial glide towards suitable country, if necessary, whether or not it is to be lowered finally.

iii) Approach and land in the normal way, as described in para. 44. Flaps may be left up until after turning in towards the field, in order that the pilot can hold them in reserve - the aeroplane tends to overshoot (flaps up) and then, at the right moment, flaps are lowered. The aeroplane sideslips with flaps down quite affectively, and is, therefore, not difficult to land accurately in a forced landing without assistance of engine.

A.P.1565B, Vol.I, Sect.2

POSITION ERROR TABLE

54. The corrections for position error are as follows:-

At 300 m.p.h. A.S.I. reading subtract	$8\frac{1}{2}$ m.p.h.
" 280 " " " "	$8\frac{1}{2}$ "
" 260 " " " "	$9\frac{1}{2}$ "
" 240 " " " "	8 "
" 220 " " " "	$7\frac{1}{2}$ "
" 200 " " " "	6 "
" 180 " " " "	$3\frac{1}{2}$ "
" 160 " " " "	1 "
" 140 " " " add	3 "
" 120 " " " "	7 "

NOTES CONCERNING THE MERLIN XII ENGINE

(Rated altitude 13,000 ft.- Fuel 100 octane)

55. The following should be carefully noted:-

(i) <u>Limiting operational conditions.</u>-

Take-off (up to 1,000 ft. or for 3 mins.)	Maximum r.p.m. Minimum r.p.m. at maximum boost (+12 lb./sq.in.)	3,000 2,270
Climb (30 min. periods)	Maximum r.p.m. at maximum boost (+9 lb./sq.in.)	2,850
Maximum cruising (Mixture control NORMAL)	Maximum r.p.m. at maximum boost (+7 lb./sq.in.)	2,650
Maximum cruising (mixture control WEAK)	Maximum r.p.m. at maximum boost ($+3\frac{3}{4}$ lb./sq.in.)	2,650
All-out level (5 mins. limit)	Maximum r.p.m. at maximum boost (+9 lb./sq.in.)	3,000
Maximum dive (20 seconds limit)	Momentary maximum r.p.m. at maximum boost (+ 9 lb./sq.in.)	3,600

F.S./16

(ii) **Oil pressures.-**

Normal	60 lb./sq.in.
Emergency minimum	45 lb./sq.in.

(iii) **Oil inlet temperatures.-**

Minimum for opening up	15°C.
Maximum for continuous cruising	90°C.
Maximum for climbing	90°C.
Emergency maximum	95°C.

(iv) **Coolant temperature.-** The engine which employs an ethylene glycol solution as the cooling medium, should not be opened up to full power until the radiator temperature exceeds 60°C. The maximum permissible temperature in flight is 120°C. and the recommended cruising temperature should not exceed 100°C.

FUEL AND OIL CAPACITY AND CONSUMPTIONS

56. Note the following:-

(i) **Oil capacity.-** The oil tank has a total capacity of 7.5 gallons and an effective capacity of 5.8 gallons.

(ii) **Effective fuel capacity.-**

Two main tanks - top tank .... 48 gallons
bottom tank .... 37 gallons
Total effective capacity 85 gallons

(iii) **Fuel consumptions.-** The following information will be found useful in determining endurances:-

Maximum fuel consumptions (at altitudes stated)

Climbing - 2,850 r.p.m.	93.5 gallons per hour at 13,000 ft.
All-out level - 3,000 r.p.m.	98 gallons per hour at 14,500 ft.
Maximum cruising (mixture control NORMAL) - 2,650 r.p.m.	77.5 gallons per hour at 13,000 ft.
Maximum cruising (mixture control WEAK) - 2,650 r.p.m.	55.5 gallons per hour at 18,000 ft.

May 1942
AIR MINISTRY

Amendment List No.23/J.
to
AIR PUBLICATION 1565B,
Volume I and
Pilot's Notes.

SPITFIRE IIA & IIB AEROPLANES
MERLIN XII ENGINE.

Note: Amendment Lists to this Air Publication which affect the Pilot's Notes are now allotted a letter as well as a number. The letters will run consecutively, omitting I and O. The Pilot's Notes will be complete if the following "current" amendment lists have been incorporated; these have been allotted the letters shown:

8	10	19	22	23
A	B	F	H	J

(1) SECTION 2 — Para.5(v). **Delete** "100" and **substitute** "150".

(2) SECTION 2 — Para.5. Mark end of this paragraph **to refer** to this sheet and **note** the following: "When engines are being kept warm in readiness for immediate take-off, de Havilland 20° C.S. propeller should be left in fine pitch - control lever fully forward".

(3) SECTION 2 — Remove existing sheets bearing Paras.12 to 20 and substitute new sheets supplied herewith.

(4) SECTION 2 — Remove Amendment List No.16 and **insert** this sheet at end of Section as authority for the above amendments.

R.T.P./1323

IN HIGH DEFINITION
NOW AVAILABLE!

COMPLETE LINE OF WWII AIRCRAFT FLIGHT MANUALS

www.PERISCOPEFILM.COM

©2012 Periscope Film LLC
All Rights Reserved
ISBN#978-1-937684-68-6

www.ingramcontent.com/pod-product-compliance
Lightning Source LLC
Chambersburg PA
CBHW070654050426
42451CB00008B/350